The Book of FASCINATING FACTS

The Book of FASCINATING FACTS

An indispensable modern miscellany

JOHN BLAKE

Published by John Blake Publishing Ltd,
3 Bramber Court, 2 Bramber Road,
London W14 9PB, England

www.blake.co.uk

First published in hardback in 2007

ISBN 978 1 84454 487 5

British Library Cataloguing-in-Publication Data:

A catalogue record for this book is available from the British Library.

Design by www.envydesign.co.uk
Printed and bound in Great Britain by Mackays of Chatham Ltd,
Chatham, Kent

1 3 5 7 9 10 8 6 4 2

Papers used by John Blake Publishing are natural, recyclable products made from wood grown in sustainable forests. The manufacturing processes conform to the environmental regulations of the country of origin.

CONTENTS

Chapter 1

THE BODY – BEAUTIFUL?

You probably know your height and weight. You may even know your blood group. But what else do you really know about the wonders of your body? Did you know that you produce enough saliva in a lifetime to fill two swimming pools, or that you blink more than 6 million times? Do you know how many taste buds there are on your tongue? Or how much you… er… poo in a year?

69: number of decibels that a human snore can reach. And you wondered why you couldn't sleep…

0.3: average time in seconds that it takes to blink. And we blink around 6,205,000 times in a lifetime.

2st 11lb (17.6kg): amount of dead skin shed from our feet in a lifetime. That's enough to fill eighteen 1kg (2.2lb) flour bags.

700: how many times more bacteria grow in your ears because of the heat from your iPod headphones.

1.2: number of pints of sweat (0.6 litres) we lose in a day. In a lifetime, we'll sweat around 31,700 pints (18,013 litres), or 60 bathfuls.

1.7: number of pints (0.9 litres) of blood per minute that our kidneys can clean. Each day they purify 3,000 pints (1,705 litres), or three-quarters of a phone box full.

230,000: pooh! That's the number of times we break wind in a lifetime. Unless we're addicted to pickled onions, baked beans or Brussels sprouts, of course, in which case it's probably a lot more…

3.7: years will be cut from our lives by periodontal (gum) disease if we don't look after our teeth.

5: the weight in ounces (141g) of an average daily poo. Sixty-eight per cent of us go once a day and in a year poop 10lb (4.5kg). In the UK, we produce 1 million stone (6,350,293kg) of faeces a day – the same weight as the Eiffel Tower.

7: the number of bars of soap that could be made from the fat in an average human body – and the number of moles on the average body.

25–26: length in feet (7.6–7.9m) of our small intestines. They are 1.1in (2.7cm) in diameter and food passes through at a speed of 1in (2.5cm) per minute.

6.4: length in feet (1.9m) of the colon (large intestine). That's the same height as Premiership goalie David James… but far less leaky!

43: number of muscles you use to frown. You use around 17 to smile.

2,200: match heads that could be made from the amount of phosphorous in the average human body.

28: weight in grams of the average human eyeball – that's about an ounce, or the same as three £1 coins.

85: percentage of the human brain that is made up of water. It's also the number of different jobs that the liver does.

560: speed of a cough in miles per hour (901km/h). A tailwind that fast would fly you from Newcastle to London in just eight minutes.

110: speed of a sneeze in miles per hour (177km/h). That's more than one-and-a-half times the UK's national speed limit for driving.

1,800: distance in miles (2,896km) that all the willies of men over 16 in England and Wales would stretch if cut off and laid end-to-end! That's the distance from London to the Canary Islands. If they were erect, they would stretch 4,000 miles (6,437km), or from London to Chicago.

10,000: number of taste buds on our tongues, each containing 50 taste cells.

50,000: pints (28,400 litres) of spit produced in a lifetime – enough to fill two swimming pools.

60,000: the length in miles (9.656km) of all our

blood vessels. If they were placed end-to-end, they would stretch the distance that the Earth travels around the Sun in an hour.

100,000: the total number of hairs on the average human scalp.

600,000: particles of skin shed every hour. By the age of 70, an average person will have lost 105lb (47.6kg) of skin.

32,000,000: number of bacteria that live and crawl all over every square inch of us…

3,300,000,000: total number of times that your heart beats in a lifetime.

9: total weight in pounds (4kg) of the ashes of a human being who has been cremated.

★ ★ ★ ★ ★

And if your brain's not already swimming with all those bodily facts and stats, try these for size:

£19.7 billion was spent on beer by thirsty Britons in 2005. That's 228 pints per person.

180 million sperm are ejaculated at one time. Four hours later, 60 per cent are still alive and 15 per cent survive a whole 24 hours.

100 million nerve cells exist in the human body. If you tried to count them one every second it would take you more than THREE YEARS.

32 million bacteria live on every square inch of our bodies.

722,500 babies were born in Britain last year. The record high was in 1920, with 1.13 million births – a reaction to the losses of World War I.

£8,000 cash will buy a cornea to be used for a transplant operation for wealthy buyers to regain their sight.

100,000 muscle movements are made by one eyeball every day – making our eyes our busiest muscles.

£24,000 is what wealthy patients will pay for a new liver on the black market. Advances in medical technology mean the liver in a living person can now be split up and part of it sold. The remainder will re-grow.

22,000 tons (22,352 tonnes) of chips are eaten each week in the UK.

10,000 people are aged 100 or over in Britain. By 2075, this figure is expected to increase to a massive 1.2 million.

£220 is the price of human eggs on the black market.

149 is the average number of times an adult has sex each year.

76 years is the average life expectancy of a UK man. For women, it's 86. People in Bury St Edmunds, Suffolk have the highest life expectancy, with 93.4 years. Middlesbrough has the lowest, with just 67.8 years.

50 tons (50,802kg) of food will pass through your digestive system in your lifetime. That's nearly the weight of two fully-grown humpback whales.

35 days are needed to grow an eyelash.

30 is the average age of marriage for a man. It's 28 for women.

27.3 is the average age at which a woman has her first baby. The average first time dad is aged 29.

45 miles (72km) of nerves exist in our skin. If placed end to end, they would stretch all the way from London to Brighton.

20 seconds is the length of the average dream and we have about four of them every night – that's around 1,460 every year, a bit like watching around five full-length films.

12 hours is the average time it takes for a person to digest a whole Sunday roast dinner.

3 pounds (1.36 kg) is the average weight of a human brain. It has a storage capacity of more than four terabytes – that's 4,194, 304 megabytes, or about the same as almost 3 million standard computer floppy discs.

1.7 children is the average number per couple, not the 2.4 that most people and comedy sitcom writers think.

Chapter 2

ALL CREATURES GREAT AND SMALL

Now you know how much your eyeballs weigh and how many bugs live on your skin, we thought you should know how you measure up to animals. Did you know that crocodiles can't stick their tongues out, ants never sleep and gorillas have tiny willies?

Earwigs have two penises, each longer than the earwig itself. They are also very fragile and easily snap off, which is why the insect is born with a spare.

A pregnant camel is known as a git.

The first animal to be sent into space was a fruit fly – on the USA's 1946 V2 expedition.

All polar bears are left-handed, but dogs and cats, like humans, are either right- or left-handed… or is that left-pawed?

The blue whale is the planet's largest mammal, weighing 50 tons (50,802kg) at birth and 150 tons (152,407kg) fully grown. It is also the loudest, with a whistle of 188 decibels – louder than a jet at take-off.

A male pig's orgasm lasts for 15 minutes.

A gorilla's penis is just one-and-a-quarter inches (3.17cm) long.

A crocodile cannot stick its tongue out.

Goats and octopuses have rectangular pupils in their eyes.

Cats' urine glows in the dark.

Polar bear livers are poisonous because they contain so much vitamin C.

Males ducks – also known as drakes – take part in group sex after ambushing a lone female… often drowning her in the process.

A chameleon tongue is twice the length of its body.

The giant squid has the largest eyes of any animal. They can be 15 inches (39cm) across, which is sixteen times wider than the average human eye.

A rat can last longer without water than a camel.

A Jellyfish is 95 per cent water.

Elephants spend 23 hours a day eating.

Dolphins sleep with one eye open.

An ostrich's eye is bigger than its brain.

One golden poison-dart frog has enough venom in it to kill up to 1,500 people.

Vultures sometimes eat so much they can't take off again.

The Jesus Christ lizard that lives in the Amazon can run across water.

Bluebottle flies can smell meat from 4 miles (6.4km) away.

Many birds migrate long distances, but the Arctic tern travels furthest. It flies from the Arctic to the Antarctic and back again every year – a round trip of 20,000 miles (32,186km).

A peregrine falcon can spot its prey from more than 5 miles (8km) away.

A woodpecker can peck twenty times a second.

Frogs have an eardrum on the outside of their head, and crickets have ears on their front legs.

A zebra is white with black stripes – and no two have the exact same patterns.

The sleepiest mammals are armadillos, sloths and opossums. They spend 80 per cent of their lives sleeping or dozing.

Chimpanzees, which are apes, can learn to recognise themselves in a mirror. Monkeys can't.

Sea otters always float on their backs when they eat.

Snakes can see through their eyelids.

The world's largest rodent is the capybara, a semi-aquatic native of South America. It grows to 2ft (60cm) tall and weighs around 9 stones (57kg).

Cobras can kill with a bite as soon as they are born.

A giraffe has the same number of bones in its neck as a human.

A cat sees six times better than a human at night because of the tapetum lucidum – a layer of extra reflecting cells in its eyes that absorb light.

Baby amarobia spiders eat their mothers when they are born.

Cows give nearly 200,000 glasses of milk in a lifetime.

Porpoises and dolphins communicate with each other by squeaking, growling, moaning and whistling.

A bed usually houses more than 6 billion dust mites.

More people are killed every year by donkeys than die in air crashes.

A shrimp's heart is in its head.

The hippopotamus gives birth under water and nurses its young in a river, although the young hippos do come up for air from time to time.

The world's smallest mammal is the bumblebee bat of Thailand, weighing less than a 1 pence piece.

A pistol shrimp surprises its prey by banging its claws together loudly to put it off guard.

A cockroach can live for nine days once its head has been cut off – and only dies because it can't eat or drink.

A female cod can lay up to 9 million eggs in a single spawning.

Starfish can grow a new arm if one is damaged, and slowworms and lizards can re-grow broken-off tails.

Chapter 3

THE WRITING'S ON THE WALL

For as long as there have been walls, man has scrawled on them. From scratches in prehistoric caves to today's spray-paint graffiti over everything from train carriages to public lavatories, here is a selection of real-life messages.

Lost – wife and dog. Reward for dog.

I went to buy some camouflage trousers the other day but I couldn't find any.

(On the back of a grubby white van) I wish my wife was as dirty as this.

OK, so what's the speed of dark?

What happens if you get scared half to death twice?

If one synchronised swimmer drowns, do they all have to?

Why don't sheep shrink when it rains?

What did the inventor of the drawing board go back to?

If a pig loses its voice, is it disgruntled?

What was the best thing before sliced bread?

I went to San Francisco. I found someone's heart. Now what?

Why do they lock petrol station toilets? Are they afraid someone will clean them?

(In a pet shop) Buy one dog at the regular price and get one flea.

Borrow money from pessimists – they don't expect it back.

How can there be self-help groups?

What's another word for thesaurus?

Why is it that when we talk to God we're said to be praying, but when God talks to us we're schizophrenic?

I once chatted up a cheetah. I thought I'd like to pull a fast one.

I've had amnesia for as long as I can remember.

Why isn't the number eleven pronounced onety-one?

Grow your own dope – plant a politician.

INSULTS AND ABUSE

The only curve on my wife's body is her Adam's Apple.

She's been boarded more times than the Orient Express.

My wife has looks that turn heads... and stomachs too.

Stop global warming. Shut your mouth!

My husband never drinks unless he's alone or with someone.

You're a real Action Man: crew cut, realistic scar, no genitals.

My wife has a new form of exercise – aerobic nagging.

He's nobody's fool. He freelances.

If I said you had a beautiful body, would you sue me for slander?

I find her breath offensive. It's keeping her alive.

IN THE GENTS

A clear conscience is usually the sign of a bad memory.

There are two sides to every divorce. Yours and Ratbag's.

Beauty is in the eye of the beer holder.

To pee, or not to pee, that is the question.

Express Lane: five beers or less.

Notice to all men. We aim to please. You aim too please. The Management.

Be careful – your family's future is in your hands.

My wife wasn't born yesterday… nobody could get that ugly in 24 hours.

Do you know the Watford turn-off? Yes, I married her.

'I am' is reportedly the shortest sentence in the English language. 'I do' is the longest sentence.

Support bacteria. They're the only culture some people have.

IN THE LADIES

A woman's rule of thumb: If it has tyres or testicles, you're going to have trouble with it.

How many roads must a man walk down before he admits that he's lost?

Sometimes I wake up grumpy. Other times I let him sleep.

It's not the size that counts, it's the… umm… er… actually, it is the size…

The best form of birth control after 50 is nudity.

Shin – a device for finding furniture in the dark.

Give a man a fish and he will eat for a day. Teach a man to fish and he will sit in a boat drinking beer all day.

Last night sex was so good that even the neighbours had a cigarette afterwards.

Inside me there's a thin woman crying to get out… but I can usually shut the bitch up with biscuits.

Chapter 4

DID YOU KNOW?

How many new things did you learn last year? Each week, hundreds of questions from inquiring minds seek out the answers to the burning enquiries of the day on the Internet and from our most trusted news sources such as the BBC. The results make for some amazing facts, some mind-boggling statistics, as well as some totally useless trivia.

One in ten Europeans is allegedly conceived in an Ikea bed. Every Sunday, hundreds of thousands of us visit an Ikea store – as many as 33 million people last year alone.

Restaurant is the word that is most often spelled incorrectly on search engines.

Giant squid eat each other – especially during sex.

Britain produces 700 different regional cheeses – more even than France.

Baboons can tell the difference between English and French. Zoo keepers at Port Lympne wild animal park in Kent are having to learn French after some baboons were transferred there from Paris Zoo. They found the monkeys didn't come when they called 'Dinner' in English, but when they used French words like '*Déjeuner*', the baboons came running.

Actress Nicole Kidman is scared of butterflies. 'I can jump out of planes, I can be covered in cockroaches, I do all sorts of things, but I just don't like the feel of butterflies' bodies,' she says.

It's possible for humans to blow up balloons with their ears. A 55-year-old factory worker from China discovered 20 years ago that air leaked from his ears and he can inflate balloons and blow out candles.

If all the Smarties eaten in one year were laid end to end, the line would stretch 63,380 miles (102,000km) – more than two-and-a-half times around the Earth's equator. Some 570,000 tubes are made every day, each containing 48 sweets, and in the UK 307 tubes are eaten every minute.

The equals sign (=) was invented by 16th-century Welsh mathematician Robert Recorde, who was fed up writing 'is equal to' in his equations. He chose the two lines because 'noe 2 thynges can be moare equalle'.

Britons buy more CDs than anyone in the world – an average of 3.2 per year, compared to 2.8 in the US and 2.1 in France.

Traffic cones were first used in building Preston bypass in the late 1950s. Before then, workmen put out red lantern paraffin burners.

The London borough of Westminster has an average of twenty pieces of chewing gum on every square metre of pavement.

The average employee spends fourteen working days a year, not counting official breaks, on personal emails, phone calls and web browsing.

Legendary Tour De France cyclist Lance Armstrong's heart is almost a third larger than the average man's.

A towel doesn't legally reserve a sun lounger and there is nothing in German or Spanish law to stop other holidaymakers moving those left to reserve sunbeds.

One person in four has had their identity stolen or knows someone else who has.

When celebrity couple Brad Pitt and Jennifer Aniston split up, Madame Tussaud's had a problem. Their waxworks were joined together... It was the first time the museum had two waxworks joined and may be the last, as it cost them £10,000 to separate the pair.

The man who was the voice of one of the original Daleks, Roy Skelton, also did the voices for George and Zippy in children's TV series *Rainbow*.

Oliver Twist is very popular in China, where its title translates as 'Foggy City Orphan'.

WD-40 – the magic spray that gets cars going – also dissolves cocaine. It has been used by a pub landlord to stop drug taking in his pub's toilets.

New York Mayor Michael Bloomberg's home number is listed by directory inquiries.

One in 18 people has a third nipple.

One in six children thinks that broccoli is a baby tree.

Fifty-seven Bic biros are sold every second – making a total of 100 billion sold since 1950.

Friday 16 March 2001 is the only day in the ten years between 1993 and 2002 when no one committed suicide in the UK. It is also the day when comedian Jack Dee won *Celebrity Big Brother.*

Chelsea boss Jose Mourinho has been in an English pub only once – when he popped in to buy his wife cigarettes.

Pulling your foot out of quicksand takes the same force as it would take to lift a medium-sized car.

Croydon has more CCTV cameras than New York.
You are 176 times more likely to be murdered than to win the National Lottery.

In America, it's possible to force a dog to appear as a witness in a court case.

It takes 165lb (74.8kg) of raw materials to make one mobile phone.

Newborn dolphins and killer whales don't sleep for the first month of their lives, according to researchers at the University of California.

Jimi Hendrix pretended to be gay to get out of the US Army.

An average Briton will spend £1,537,380 during his or her lifetime.

Britain's smallest church, near Malmesbury, Wiltshire, opens just once a year. It measures 13ft (3.9m) by 12ft (3.6m) and has one pew.

Chapter 5

THAT'S AMORE!

For many of us, the final stop on the love train is the wedding. But not all marriages go as planned and some people have strange views about the institution.

The term 'best man' dates back to the times when Scotsmen used to kidnap their future brides. The friend of the groom who had excelled at the abduction was classed as the 'best' man.

The longest ever recorded marriage was that of Sir Temulji Nariman and his wife Lady Nariman, who wed at the age of five in India in 1853. The couple were married for 86 years.

History's most famous lothario, Casanova, almost married his own daughter. He asked for the hand of a pretty girl named Leonilda, but her mother screamed and fainted when introduced to her future son-in-law. She was one of Casanova's conquests, and had borne his child seventeen years earlier.

The people of the Czech Republic throw peas at weddings instead of rice. And Italians throw sugared almonds

Shakespeare famously wrote: 'Many a good hanging prevents a bad marriage.'

A Mexico City couple who didn't believe in rushing things got married in 1969 – after an engagement that lasted an incredible 67 years. Both were 82 when they finally took the plunge.

The biggest ever wedding attendance was for a Jewish ceremony in Jerusalem in 1993, when 30,000 guests helped the couple celebrate.

Before the last century, rich Egyptian men preferred not to deflower their brides personally. Instead they hired a servant to undertake the chore.

Hollywood stars Catherine Zeta-Jones and Michael Douglas spent £500 per guest just for the food at their New York wedding in November 2000.

'There's only one way to have a happy marriage and as soon as I learn what it is I'll get married again.' – Clint Eastwood

Glamour babe Jordan said before her wedding to Peter Andre: 'I want to look a bit covered-up and virginal. Pete knows what's underneath, I suppose, but then again so does everyone else.'

The word 'bride' comes from the ancient German Teutonic word for a cook.

The longest British marriage has been between Bill Jones, 105, and his Eluned, 102. The couple, from Slough, Berkshire, have been wed for 83.5 years. They have a son of 83, a granddaughter, two great-grandchildren and a great-great grandson.

Sex symbol Marilyn Monroe once said: 'Before marriage, a girl has to make love to a man to hold him. After marriage, she has to hold him to make love to him.'

Elizabethan wedding customs decreed that with parental permission it was legal for boys to marry at fourteen and girls at twelve.

A wedding veil was originally worn by Roman brides. It was thought it would disguise the bride and outwit evil spirits.

The oldest recorded bride was Minnie Munro, who got hitched at a sprightly 102. Minnie, from Australia, wed a toy boy aged 82.

Austin Powers star Mike Myers one commented: 'Marriage can be viewed as the waiting room for death.'

Multi-millionaire Peter Shalson and wife Pauline paid a record £2 million to get Elton John to sing at their wedding.

George IV got so drunk on the day of his wedding to Caroline of Brunswick that he had to be carried to the altar.

The most expensive wedding was held in a purpose-built stadium in Dubai for a Sheikh's son. The wedding cost £22 million – and lasted an amazing seven days.

Every day, 26,000 couples get married in China.

In 1976, Los Angeles secretary Jannene Swift officially married a 50lb (22.6kg) rock. The ceremony was witnessed by more than twenty people.

The longest wedding dress train was found in Germany – it was 515ft (160m) long.

In ancient Poland, it was believed that sprinkling sugar on the bride's bouquet kept her temper sweet.

In the largest ever mass wedding, 21,000 couples from the Moonie cult married on the same day.

Singer Cher opined: 'The trouble with some women is that they get all excited about nothing, then marry him.'

Whenever movie star Joan Crawford changed husbands, she changed all the toilet seats in the house.

New Yorkers Richard and Carole Roble enjoyed marrying each other so much they have taken their vows 55 times. Each ceremony was held in a different location.

Leonardo Da Vinci said: 'Marriage is like putting your hand into a bag of snakes in the hope of pulling out an eel.'

Tradition dictates that a new wife must enter her home by the main door and, to avoid bad luck, must never trip or fall – hence the custom that a bride should be carried over the threshold.

In Anglo-Saxon times, a man could divorce his wife on the grounds that she was too passionate.

Saudi Arabian women literally have grounds for divorce. They can obtain a separation if their husband doesn't give them coffee.

Impotence is a reason for divorce in 24 states in the USA.

Much-wed actress Zsa Zsa Gabor said: 'A girl must marry for love, and keep on marrying till she finds it.'

Former Baptist minister Glynn Scotty Wolfe is famous for taking 28 brides and divorcing 27 of them.

The wedding tradition in Greece is to write the names of all the bride's unmarried female friends and relatives on the sole of her shoe. After the wedding, the shoe is examined – and those whose names have been worn off are said to be next in line for a journey up the aisle.

It was an Elizabethan custom that the bride would wear her best gown for her wedding. The white dress only became fashionable after Queen Victoria wore one.

'Archaeologists make the best husbands. The older you get, the more they are interested.' – Agatha Christie

THE PATH OF TRUE LOVE NEVER RUNS SMOOTH

Every Valentine's Day, lovers gaze into each other's eyes and whisper loads of daft things they'd be embarrassed to say out loud. But love doesn't always run smooth and when it goes wrong, people can get angry, sad – or just have a good laugh.

'The best way to get a husband to do anything is to say he's too old.' – Shirley Maclaine

'My wife and I always hold hands. If I let go, she shops.' – Rodney Dangerfield

'I bought my wife a sex manual, but half the pages were missing. We went straight from foreplay to post-natal depression.' – Bob Monkhouse

'The useless piece of flesh at the end of a penis is called a man.' – Jo Brand

'I was incredible in bed last night. I never once had to sit up and consult the manual.' – Woody Allen

'Never marry a man with a big head. Because you're going to give birth to that man's child and you want a baby with a narrow head.' – Jilly Goolden

'My wife said: "I want an explanation and I want the truth." I said: "Make up your mind."' – Henny Youngman

'I haven't spoken to my wife for over a month. We haven't had a row – I'm just afraid to interrupt.' – Les Dawson

'I had bad luck with both my wives. The first one left me and the second one didn't.' – Patrick Murray

'The night of our honeymoon my husband took one look and said: "Is that all for me?"' – Dolly Parton

'I didn't get too many women running after me. It was their husbands who'd be after me.' – Charlie George

'If there is reincarnation, I'd like to come back as Warren Beatty's fingertips.' – Woody Allen

'My parents had only one argument in 45 years. It lasted 43 years.' – Cathy Ladman

'My mother said it was simple to keep a man. You must be a maid in the living room, a cook in the kitchen and a whore in the bedroom. I said I'd hire the first two and take care of the bedroom bit myself.' – Jerry Hall

'I've been in love with the same woman for 40 years – if my wife ever finds out, she'll kill me.' – Henny Youngman

'I placed a personal ad in a magazine saying I wanted to meet a rich, well-insured widow with a view to murdering her. I got 48 replies.' – Spike Milligan

'My wife and I pondered whether to take a vacation or get a divorce. We decided a trip to Bermuda is over in two weeks but a divorce is something you always have.' – Woody Allen

'A woman's mind is cleaner than a man's. That's because she changes it more often.' – Oliver Herford

'I once had a large gay following, but I ducked into an alleyway and lost him.' – Emo Philips

'I am not bald. My head is just a solar panel for a sex machine.' – Telly Savalas

'I admit the most recent fight with my wife was my fault. She said: "What's on the TV?" and I said: "Dust."' – Roy Brown

'Of all the faculties, the last to leave us is sexual desire. That means long after we're wearing bifocals or hearing aids we'll still be making love. But we won't know with whom or why.' – Jack Paar

'If you think women are the weaker sex, try pulling the blankets back to your side.' – Stuart Turner

'A man should be able to change his wife like a banknote when she's forty – for two twenties.' – Douglas Jerrold

'The mini-skirt enables young ladies to run faster and, because of it, they may have to.' – John V. Lindsay

'Gay marriage will never work. It's difficult enough when you have even one man in a marriage.' – Graham Norton

'The love bird is one hundred per cent faithful to his mate – as long as they're locked in the same cage.' – Will Cuppy

'The only way to get rid of cockroaches is to tell them you want a long-term relationship.' – Jasmine Birtles

'Why does a woman work for ten years to change a man's habits and then complain he's not the man she married?' – Barbra Streisand

'Anniversaries are like toilets – men usually miss them.' – Jo Brand

'The difference between divorce and legal separation is that legal separation gives a man time to hide his money.' – Johnny Carson

'My ideal man is young, handsome and looks as if his teeth will stay in all night.' – Victoria Wood

'You know that look women have when they want to have sex? Me neither.' – Steve Martin

'I don't think my wife likes me very much. When I had a heart attack she wrote for an ambulance.' – Frank Carson

'I blame myself for my boyfriend's death. I shot him.' – Jo Brand

'Of course I believe in safe sex… I have a handrail around the bed.' – Ken Dodd

'Love is the delightful interval that comes between meeting a girl and discovering that she looks like a haddock.' – John Barrymore

'There are a number of mechanical devices which increase sexual arousal, particularly in women. Chief among these is the Mercedes-Benz 380SL convertible.' – P. J. O'Rourke

'Women may be able to fake orgasms, but men can fake whole relationships.' – Sharon Stone

LOVE IN THE LIMELIGHT

With all the multi-million pound celebrity splits that make the news, it makes you wonder how the rich and famous feel when they fall out of love. But if there's nothing you can do about it, you may as well laugh it off.

'I said to the wife: "Guess what I heard in the pub? They reckon the milkman has made love to every woman in our road except one." And she said: "I'll bet it's that stuck-up Phyllis at No 23."' – Max Kauffmann

'I married beneath me – all women do.' – Nancy Astor

'The most happy marriage I can imagine to myself would be the union of a deaf man to a blind woman.' – Samuel Taylor Coleridge

'I'd marry again if I found a man who had $15 million and would sign over half of it to me before the marriage, and guarantee he'd be dead within a year.' – Bette Davis

'In my house I'm the boss. My wife is just the decision maker.' – Woody Allen

'How marriage ruins a man. It's as demoralising as cigarettes, and far more expensive.' – Zsa Zsa Gabor

'There is one thing I would break up over and that's if she caught me with another woman. I wouldn't stand for that.' – Steve Martin

'Marrying a man is like buying something you've been admiring for a long time in a shop window. You may love it when you get it home, but it doesn't always go with everything else in the house.' – Jean Kerr

'Politics doesn't make strange bedfellows, marriage does.' – Groucho Marx

'My husband and I didn't sign a pre-nuptial agreement. We signed a mutual suicide pact.' – Roseanne Barr

'My divorce came to me as a complete surprise. That's what happens when you haven't been home in 18 years.' – Lee Trevino

'When a man brings his wife flowers for no reason, there's a reason.' – Molly McGee

'There is nothing in the world like the devotion of a married woman. It is something no married man knows anything about.' – Oscar Wilde

'I don't think I'll get married again. I'll just find a woman I don't like and give her a house.' – Lewis Grizzard

'See, the problem is that God has given men a brain and a penis, and only enough blood to run one at a time.' – Robin Williams

'I have never hated a man enough to give his diamonds back.' – Zsa Zsa Gabor

'Women need a reason to have sex. Men just need a place.' – Billy Crystal

'They say marriages are made in heaven. But so is thunder and lightning.' – Clint Eastwood

'The only charm of marriage is that it makes a life of deception necessary for both parties.' – Oscar Wilde

'For the first year of marriage I had a basically bad attitude. I tended to place my wife underneath a pedestal.' – Woody Allen

'I belong to Bridegrooms Anonymous. Whenever I feel like getting married, they send over a lady in a housecoat and hair curlers to burn my toast for me.' – Dick Martin

'The only time my wife and I had a simultaneous orgasm was when the judge signed the divorce papers.' – Woody Allen

'I told my wife the truth. I told her I was seeing a psychiatrist. Then she told me the truth… that she was seeing a psychiatrist, two plumbers and a bartender.' – Rodney Dangerfield

'Marriage is neither heaven or hell, it is simply purgatory.' – Abraham Lincoln

'Keep your eyes wide open before marriage and half shut afterwards.' – Benjamin Franklin

'It is well to be off with the old woman before you're on with the new.' – George Bernard Shaw

'I was brought up to respect the conventions, so love had to end in marriage. I'm afraid it did.' – Bette Davis

'The happiest time in any man's life is just after the first divorce.' – John Kenneth Galbraith.

'Bigamy is having one wife too many. Monogamy is the same.' – Oscar Wilde

'My boyfriend and I broke up. He wanted to get married, and I didn't want him to.' – Mae West

'Men marry women with the hope they will never change. Women marry men with the hope they will. Invariably they are both disappointed.' – Albert Einstein

'I love Mickey Mouse more than any woman I've ever known.' – Walt Disney

'Ah, yes, divorce… from the Latin word meaning to rip out a man's genitals through his wallet…' – Robin Williams

‘A man is incomplete until he is married. After that, he is finished.’ – Zsa Zsa Gabor

‘It was a perfect marriage. She didn’t want to and he couldn’t.’ – Spike Milligan

Chapter 6

JOKE CORNER

A white horse walks into a pub and asks for a whisky. The barman says: 'That is amazing, absolutely amazing! Did you know there's a whisky named after you?' The horse replies: 'You're kidding me. There's a whisky called Eric?'

A man goes into a bar with a small newt on a lead. The barman says, 'You're not bringing that thing in here.' 'Come on,' says the man, 'he's minute.'

What do you call a woman juggling beer?
Beatrix.
And playing pool?
Beatrix Potter.

Two drunks are walking along the road in London. One turns to the other and slurs, 'Is this Wembley?' 'No, it's Thursday.' 'So am I! Let's go for a drink.'

Two peanuts walk into a bar. One was a salted.

A bear goes into a pub and says, 'Can I have a pint of Guinness, please?'
The barman says, 'Sure, but why the big pause?'

A man walks into a pub with a crocodile and a chicken. He orders a pint. Then the crocodile says he'll have one too. The barman stares in amazement and says to the man: 'Wow! I've never seen that before – where did you find a talking crocodile?' The man looks at the barman and says: 'Don't be ridiculous – a talking crocodile? The chicken's a ventriloquist!'

A skeleton goes into a bar. He orders a pint of beer and a mop.

A dog with one leg walks into a western bar and says to the bartender, 'I'm looking for the man who shot my paw…'

A mushroom walks into a bar, sits down and orders a drink. The bartender says: 'I'm afraid we don't serve mushrooms here.'
'Why not? I'm a fun guy!'

A sandwich goes into a pub, walks up to the barman and says: 'Pint of lager.'
The barman replies: 'Sorry mate. We don't serve food.'

Vincent van Gogh is standing at the bar of his pub when his mate Renoir walks in and asks: 'Fancy a whisky?'
Van Gogh replies: 'No, it's OK. I've got one ear.'

A drunk walks into a bar, goes over to a woman standing at the jukebox, and grabs her bum. 'What the hell do you think you're doing?' the woman screams. 'I'm sorry,' replies the drunk. 'I thought you were my wife.'
'Why, you drunken, worthless, insufferable pig!' she yells. 'See? You sound just like her.'

A jump-lead walks into a bar. The barman says: 'I'll serve you, but don't start anything.'

A brain goes into a pub and says: 'Pint of lager.' The barman replies: 'Sorry mate, you're out of your head already.'

A woman walks into a bar and asks the barman for a double entendre – so he gives her one.

An alien goes into a packed pub and says: 'Hello Earthlings! I come in peace and as a gesture of goodwill I will buy everyone a drink!' Many drinks later, the barman says to the alien: 'OK, that'll be £248, please.' The alien replies: 'D'ya have change for a Zog?'

A neutron goes into a bar and asks the barman: 'How much for a beer?' 'For you, no charge,' the barman replies.

Lionel Richie goes into a pub and says: 'Pint of Guinness, please?' 'No problem,' says the barman, 'but why the long face?'

A giraffe walks into a bar and says: 'The hi-balls are on me.'

A pig goes into a bar, orders ten drinks and finishes them all before saying goodnight. The bartender says: 'Don't you need to use the loo first?' The pig says: 'No, I go wee wee wee all the way home.'

A kangaroo walks into a bar and orders a beer. The bartender says: 'That'll be £5. You know, we don't get many kangaroos coming in here.' The kangaroo says, 'At £5 a beer, it's not surprising.'

A guy walks into a bar and says: 'Ouch!' It was an iron bar.

A penguin walks into a bar, goes to the counter, and asks the bartender: 'Have you seen my brother?' The bartender asks: 'I don't know. What does he look like?'

A man goes into a pub and orders a double Martini on the rocks. After he finishes the drink, he peeks inside his shirt pocket, then he orders another double Martini. After he finishes that one, he again peeks inside his shirt pocket and orders another double Martini. Finally, the bartender says, 'Look, buddy, I'll bring ya Martinis all night long. But you gotta tell me why you look inside your shirt pocket before you order a refill.' The customer replies: 'I'm peeking at a photo of my wife. When she starts to look good, then I know it's time for me to go home.'

A man walks into a bar, sits down and hears a small voice say, 'You look nice today.' A few minutes later he again hears a small voice: 'That's a nice shirt.' The guy asks the barman, 'Who is that?' The barmen says: 'The peanuts. They're complimentary!'

Shakespeare walks into a bar and asks for a beer. 'I'm sorry, but I can't serve you,' says the bartender. 'You're Bard!'

While driving along the back roads of a small town, two truckers come to a low bridge with a sign that reads CLEARANCE 11ft 3in. They get out and measure their lorry, which is 12ft 4in high. 'What do you think?' one asks the other. The driver looks around carefully, then he jumps in the cab and starts the engine. 'Not a cop in sight,' he says. 'Let's take a chance!'

Playing poker online is like being mugged … but without the company.

How do crazy people walk through a forest?
They use the psychopath.

I sent my daughter to a private school. That's 73 grand's worth of education, and now she wants to be an actor… So I've asked her to do porn and give me the money back.

What goes: Ha ha ha clonk?
A man laughing his head off.

I got an odd-job man in. He was useless. I gave him a list of eight things to do and he only did numbers one, three, five and seven. I had to get an even-job man in to do the rest.

If you're chased by a police dog, don't go through a tunnel, then on to a little see-saw, then jump through a hoop of fire. They're trained for that.

How do you get the attention of fat people? Piece of cake.

'My friend is Irish.'
'Oh really?'
'O'Reilly, actually.'

You have to remember all the trivia your girlfriend tells you, because eventually you get tested. She'll go: 'What's my favourite flower?' And you murmur to yourself: 'Heck, I wasn't listening… Self-raising?'

A dog goes into a hardware store and says: 'I'd like a job, please.'

The hardware store owner says: 'We don't hire dogs. Why don't you go join the circus?'
The dog replies: 'What would the circus want with a plumber?'

I like to go into the Body Shop and shout out really loudly: 'I've already got one!'

How many members of U2 does it take to change a light bulb?
Just Bono... he holds it and the world revolves around him.

I come from a very traditional family. When I was seven, my Uncle Terry hanged himself on Christmas Eve. My family didn't take his body down until the sixth of January.

I'm still making love at 71, which is handy for me 'cos I live at Number 63.

After her accident, my nan had a plastic hip put in. But I thought they should have replaced it with a Slinky, 'cos if she did fall down the stairs again...

What do you call an Aussie girl with chalk on her head? A Barbie-cue.

Americans only re-elected George Bush to prove they had a sense of irony.

I saw that Lee Majors the other day. Looked a million dollars – he's really let himself go…

'Doctor, doctor! I have a problem. I can't stop singing "The Green Green Grass Of Home" and "Delilah."'
'Sounds like you have a severe case of Tom Jones Syndrome.'
'Is that rare?'
'No, it's not unusual.'

In the Bible, God made it rain for 40 days and 40 nights. That's a pretty good summer for us in Wales. I was eight before I realised you could take a kagoule off.

What did the slug say to the snail?
'*Big Issue*, mate?'

My dad is Irish and my mum is Iranian, which meant that we spent most of our family holidays in customs.

Two guys came knocking at my door once and said: 'We want to talk to you about Jesus.' I said: 'Oh, no, what's he done now?'

Cats have nine lives. Which makes them ideal for experimentation.

I like the Ten Commandments but I have a problem with the ninth. It should be: 'Thou shalt not covet thy neighbour's ox, except in Scrabble.'

I've got no problem buying tampons. I'm a modern man. But apparently, they're not a 'proper present'.

Why do women insist on asking men what they're thinking? We're thinking: 'S★★★, better think of something to say.'

Two aerials on a roof fell in love and got married. The wedding wasn't great but the reception was fantastic.

My body has changed so much since I've been here. My stomach is fat from the food and booze, my legs are skinny from walking up all the hills. I've decided ET wasn't from outer space. He was from Edinburgh!

A hotel mini-bar allows you to see into the future – and what a can of cola will cost in 2020.

I saw a poster for *Mission Impossible III* and I thought: 'It's not really impossible if he's already done it twice.'

They say being a hostage is difficult. But I could do it with my hands tied behind my back.

Prison governor: 'Ladies, I'll turn this place into *Midnight Express*.'
Prisoner: 'Oh, I should tell you now, I'm no good on roller skates.'

'Do you smoke?'
'Only when I'm set on fire.'

Chapter 7

FOR EGGHEADS EVERYWHERE

Do you know why we give choccie treats to celebrate the Christian festival of Easter – or how much we shell out each year? Come to think of it, why are normal eggs such a popular food and an endless source of fascination?

Chocolate Easter eggs first appeared in the early 19th century in France and Germany. In the UK, J.S. Fry (now owned by Cadbury) produced its first Easter eggs in 1873. They were made of dark chocolate and filled with sweets.

A fresh egg will sink in water. A stale one will float.

The longest throw of a fresh egg – without breaking it – is 98.51m (107yd 2ft), recorded in Texas in 1978.

Places with eggy names include Egg bei Zurich (a Swiss municipality), Isle of Egg (Scottish Inner Hebrides), Eggington (near Leighton Buzzard, Bedfordshire) and Egg Harbor (New Jersey, USA).

The fastest omelette maker is American egg-centric Howard Helmer, who can rustle up 427 omelettes in 30 minutes.

In the UK, we eat 10,234 million hens' eggs a year – that's 28 million a day. Placed end to end, they would reach from the Earth to the Moon.

Eggs have been a symbol of springtime festivals since pagan times, when they represented the rebirth of the Earth after a long, hard winter. Christians changed the symbolism to mark the rebirth of man – and likened it to the tomb from which Christ rose.

In 1883, Russian Tsar Alexander asked goldsmith Peter Fabergé to make a special Easter gift for his wife, the Empress Marie. She was so thrilled that the

Tsar ordered one to be delivered every Easter. Fifty-seven were made in total.

Decorating eggs dates from the Middle Ages. In 1290, King Edward I paid 18 pence for 450 eggs to be gold-leafed and coloured as Easter gifts.

The Lion Mark for quality on eggshells was launched in 1998. Around 85 per cent of UK eggs are now produced to Lion Quality standards.

In 1997, Thai cooks thought they had made a world-record omelette, with almost 21,000 eggs – but some Japanese cooks had made one with 160,000 eggs three years earlier.

Polish legend claims the Virgin Mary gave eggs to the soldiers at the foot of Christ's cross, begging them to be less cruel. As she wept, her tears fell on the eggs, spotting them with dots of colour.

White eggs are produced by hens with white feathers. Brown eggs are produced by hens with red feathers.

Easter eggs make up eight per cent of annual chocolate sales in Britain, with more than 80 million sold annually. Worldwide, the Cadbury's Creme Egg is the most popular variety, with more than 300 million made each year.

The world record for the biggest egg-and-spoon race was set at Raynes Park High School, south London, on 24 October 2003, when 859 pupils ran 100m and finished with their eggs in one piece on their spoons.

Nursery rhyme legend Humpty Dumpty was not an egg but a large Royalist cannon on the walls above St Mary's Church, Colchester, Essex, in the Civil War. When a Roundhead cannonball hit the wall under it, Humpty fell to the ground and 'all the King's Horses and all the King's Men couldn't put Humpty together again'

Boiled eggs are the most popular way to eat eggs in Britain, followed by scrambled and fried.

In China, babies aren't officially named until they are a month old, when a Red Egg Party is held. Eggs hard-boiled and dyed red for luck are given to guests.

In the UK, eggs are graded in seven sizes, but the average one weighs 1.9–2.2 oz (53–63g).

The stringy white bit of a raw egg is called the 'chalazae'.

China produces most eggs, at about 160 billion per year. A hen can lay about 250 eggs per year.

An eggshell has as many as 17,000 pores over its surface.

Typing the word 'egg' into internet search engine Google brings up 140,000,000 entries.

In 1988, junior Health Minister Edwina Currie said most of Britain's egg production was infected with salmonella. Sales of eggs fell by 60 per cent overnight and many egg producers went out of business. Edwina was forced to resign.

Chapter 8

FANCY THAT!

More than 2,500 left-handed people a year are killed from using products made for right-handed people.

Slugs have four noses

A jiffy is an actual unit of time – it's one hundredth of a second.

The Greek National Anthem has 158 verses.

Ketchup originated in China as a pickled fish sauce called 'ketsiap'.

Barbie the doll's full name is Barbara Millicent Roberts.

A mole can dig a tunnel 300ft (91m) long in just one night.

In Tokyo, there's so much traffic that a bicycle is faster than a car for most trips of less than 50 minutes.

In Iceland, leaving a tip for a waiter at a restaurant is considered an insult.

Until the 19th century, solid blocks of tea were used as money in Siberia.

Fish in the herring family can fart in tune.

When glass breaks, the cracks move faster than 3,000 mph (4,828km/h).

A Boeing 747 airliner holds 57,285 gallons (260,422 litres) of fuel.

There is one slot machine in Las Vegas for every eight inhabitants.

Forest fires move faster uphill than downhill.

A violin contains about 70 separate pieces of wood.

Every time you lick a stamp, you consume 1/10 of a calorie.

The human eye can see light from a candle from 30 miles (48km) away on a clear, dark night.

A group of geese on the ground is called a gaggle, but a group of geese in the air is a skein.

'Facetious' and 'abstemious' contain all the vowels in the correct order, as does 'arsenious', meaning 'containing arsenic'.

If you counted aloud for 24 hours a day, it would take 31,688 years to reach 'one trillion'.

Crocodiles have the strongest bite of all animals. A 13lb (5.8kg) American alligator has a bite force of about 3,000lb (1,360kg).

Human stomach juices contain hydrochloric acid and can dissolve a cotton handkerchief.

More people use blue toothbrushes than red ones.

All the termites in the world weigh ten times more than all the humans in the world.

The phrase 'always a bridesmaid, but never a bride' comes from an advertisement for Listerine mouthwash made in 1924.

The Earth weighs around 6,600,000,000,000,000,000,000 tons (5,940 billion billion metric tonnes).

Owls are among the only birds that can see the colour blue.

There are no words in the dictionary that rhyme with 'orange' or 'purple'.

Pope John Paul II was made an Honorary Harlem Globetrotter by the US basketball team in 2000.

About 50 bibles are sold each minute across the world.

In Kentucky, USA, it's the law that a person must take a bath once a year.

A lump of pure gold the size of a matchbox can be flattened into a sheet the size of a tennis court.

It takes glass one million years to decompose.

A barnacle has the largest penis of any animal in relation to its size.

An artist from Chicago named Dwight Kalb created a statue of Madonna made out of 180lb (81.6kg) of ham.

The hash key (#) on the keyboard is called an octothorpe.

Lachanophobia is the fear of vegetables.

Camels have three eyelids to protect them from blowing sand.

There are 18 different animal shapes in the Animal Crackers cookie zoo.

Chapter 9

FINGERS CROSSED...

BRITAIN is a nation obsessed by superstition – well, it's unlucky not to be, isn't it? But why do we throw spilt salt over our shoulders, refuse to walk under ladders and get scared of magpies? And how do different parts of the country vary their beliefs?

Touching wood: Pagans believed that good spirits lived in trees – and by knocking on wood we could call on them for help.

Bird droppings: Bizarrely, if a bird poohs on your clothes or head, it means good luck – for your dry-cleaners, at least... Originally, only dove droppings gave good fortune, because the birds represented peace and friendship.

Smashing a mirror brings seven years bad luck: Comes from the days when it would cost a servant seven years' wages to buy another.

Lucky hare's foot: It was believed witches could turn themselves into hares, and carrying a hare's foot countered their power.

Putting new shoes on the table: This means someone in your family will die, it's said. It dates from the time when corpses – who were always dressed in new outfits – were laid out on a table during mourning.

Walking under a ladder: Christians believed the Holy Trinity – represented by a triangle – should not be violated by walking through it. If you do walk under a ladder, not speaking until you see a four-legged animal is meant to cancel the curse.

Nose: If your nose itches you'll hear some news – the left side means it'll be bad, the right side good.

Stepping on cracks in the pavement: This comes from an old rhyme: 'Step on a crack, break your mother's back.'

A bird flying into your home: Can signify a death because the soul is represented by a bird, which flies away out of the body when a person dies.

Ears tingling: When the right ear tingles someone is speaking well of you, but the left means the opposite. If your right ear burns, your mother is thinking of you... your left means it's your lover.

Getting out of the wrong side of the bed: By getting into bed on one side at night and up out of the other in the morning, you create a protective magic circle. Not to do so is bad luck.

Spilling salt: It used to be expensive, so spilling it was a waste. Throwing some over your left shoulder sends it into the eyes of the Devil, who sits there.

Unlucky 13: Judas – who betrayed Jesus – was the 13th person to arrive at the Last Supper.

Itchy feet: An itching on the sole of the foot means you'll soon be walking on strange ground.

Itchy hands: If your right hand itches, it means money on the way… but if your left is itchy, that means you'll have to pay for something.

Opening an umbrella indoors: Umbrellas were originally used mainly as sunshades, and opening them indoors was an insult to the sun. Some say goblins live inside furled umbrellas and will escape into the house.

First cuckoo: When you hear the first cuckoo, turn over any money in your pocket or spit on it and it will grow.

Finding a pin: 'See a pin, pick it up, all day long you'll have good luck.' This is another superstition associated with witchcraft. Witches stuck pins in effigies to bring harm, but if you find one you reverse the magic.

Wearing clothes inside out: Wearing an item of clothing inside out, or back to front, is said to bring the wearer good luck by confusing fairies so they cannot cast magic spells.

STAR SUPERSTITION

John Lennon was superstitious about the number nine and believed it affected everything in his life.

Kylie Minogue says: 'I start each day by turning the teapot three times clockwise and once anti-clockwise.'

Tennis ace Bjorn Borg wore the same shirt, and never had sex or shaved during Wimbledon fortnight – as long as he was winning, which he did five times.

Chapter 10

ERM, I CAN EXPLAIN...

MP Mark Oaten had an affair with a male prostitute because he went bald. *Cold Feet* star James Nesbitt is a love rat because his dad never warned him about strange women. As lame excuses go, they're pretty unconvincing. But they aren't the only ones to come up with limp explanations.

When actor Rob Lowe was caught by a girlfriend in a compromising position with another woman, he came up with a limp excuse – she was, he explained, just checking his penis for snakebites.

Never mind about 'leaves on the line' and 'the wrong kind of snow', British Rail once cancelled a train because the driver was too tall. In September 2005, a 6'4" (1.9m) driver at Glasgow Central station climbed into his cab to find his seat was too high for him to see properly. When he couldn't adjust it, the 7.37am service from East Kilbride was cancelled.

Aussie spin king Shane Warne tested positive for a banned substance and was kicked out of the 2003 Cricket World Cup in disgrace. But it was all quite innocent, he claimed: his mother had simply given him the diet pill Moduretic, to help make him look less fat on TV. He was given a 12-month ban.

Randy US President Bill Clinton denied having 'sexual relations' with White House intern Monica Lewinsky in 1998, and wriggled out of it later by saying that he didn't regard oral sex as 'sexual relations'. On another occasion, he admitted using drugs in his youth. 'When I was in England I experimented with marijuana a time or two, and I didn't like it.' So he took drugs? No... 'I didn't inhale,' he insisted.

Hubby Kenneth Parks drove 14 miles (22.5km) to his mother-in-law's home in 1987 and beat her to death with a metal bar. At his trial, though, he came up with a story that the jury believed and he was acquitted. He had, he said, been sleepwalking.

Darts player Mervyn King lost to Raymond Barneveld in the semi-final of the 2003 World Championships because of the air conditioning. 'It didn't affect Raymond,' he moaned later, 'because he throws a heavier dart and a very flat dart.'

Sri Lanka's cricketers put their defeat against Pakistan in the 2001 ICC Champions Trophy final down to their kit. It was too tight, they said. 'We had to add extensions to the trousers and the shirts looked more like tight-fitting women's blouses,' complained skipper Sanath Jayasuriya.

Actress Winona Ryder was only obeying orders when she was arrested for shoplifting in New York's Saks Fifth Avenue store. She told a security guard she was preparing for a movie role saying. 'I was told that I should shoplift. The director said I should try it out.'

Finnish javelin thrower Paula Huhtaniemi was woeful in the 2004 Athens Olympics, but there was a good reason. 'The big stadium surprised me,' she said. 'I couldn't direct the javelin right.'

Asked about the 'goal' he put in with his hand when Argentina beat England in the 1986 World Cup semi-final, soccer cheat Diego Maradona said it had, in fact, been scored by the 'hand of God'.

In 1999, John 'Two Jags' Prescott had to explain why his driver whisked him 250yd (228m) from his hotel to the Labour Party conference in Bournemouth. Was he being lazy? Not a bit of it. 'My wife Pauline doesn't like having her hair blown about,' he explained.

Tory battleaxe Christine Hamilton escaped a speeding fine after telling a court she 'couldn't remember' who was driving her car. The *I'm A Celebrity* star and wife of former MP Neil Hamilton was accused of speeding through 50mph (80km/h) motorway roadworks at 63mph (101km/h). Her Rover Sterling Auto was snapped by speed cameras on the M62 in Cheshire in November 2003. But, defending herself at Manchester Magistrates Court, Mrs Hamilton, 53, said she could not recall who was at the wheel when the offence took place – her or Neil. She told the judge that she and her husband covered 30,000 miles (48,280km) every year and shared the driving. 'It is pretty difficult to remember who was driving on any particular journey,' she said.

POLITICAL PRATFALLS

When it comes to claiming the title of dippiest politician on the block, there is no shortage of contenders.

'I have orders to be awakened at any time in case of a national emergency, even if I'm in a cabinet meeting.' – President Ronald Reagan

'There are more crimes in Britain now, due to a huge rise in the crime rate.' – Neil Kinnock MP

'I want to wrong that right.' – John Prescott MP

'Cod are not great swimmers so they are easily overtaken by trawlers.' – Government report on why cod are disappearing

'It's nice to be in Devon again.' – Paddy Ashdown MP… on a visit to Cornwall

'The government should provide fundamentals, like underwear, for the people at the bottom of society.' – Roy Hattersley MP

'Homelessness is homelessness, no matter where you live.' – Glenda Jackson MP

'People in the North die of ignorance and crisps.' – Edwina Currie MP

'If capitalism depended on the intellectual quality of the Conservative Party, it would end about lunchtime tomorrow.' – Tony Benn MP

'If you let that sort of thing go on, your bread and butter will be cut from right underneath your feet.' – Former PM Ernest Bevin

'I think Consett is one of the major centres for disposable baby nappies.' – Kenneth Clarke in 1995. The nappy factory closed in 1991

'At Consett, you have one of the best steelworks in Europe. It doesn't employ as many people as it used to because it's so modern.' – Kenneth Clarke MP in 1995. The steelworks had closed in 1980

'I would say the best moment of all was when I caught a 7.5lb large-mouth bass in my lake.' – President George W. Bush on his best moment in office

'I am not quite certain what my Right Honourable friend said, but we hold precisely the same view.' – PM Margaret Thatcher

'At least fifty per cent of the population are women, and the rest men.' – Harriet Harman MP

'I invented the internet.' – Former US vice president Al Gore

'We're sending 23 million leaflets to every household in Britain.' – Norman Fowler MP

'Belgium is a country invented by the British to annoy the French.' – French president Charles de Gaulle

'Traditionally most of Australia's imports come from overseas.' – Former Australian cabinet minister Keppel Enderbery

'The problem with AIDS is – you got it, you die. So why are we spending money on the issue?' – Lieutenant Governor Dennis Rehberg of Montana

'Of course it's great to see Paul Gascoigne starting at the other team's goal and running the whole length of the field to score.' – Harriet Harman MP

'It's a time of sorrow and sadness when we lose a loss of life.' – President George W. Bush

'Illegitimacy is something we should talk about in terms of not having it.' – Dan Quayle, former US vice president

Interviewer: How do you explain this huge rise in crime?
Douglas Hurd MP: There's so much more to nick.

'I'm not worried about the deficit in the budget. It is big enough to look after itself.' – President Ronald Reagan

'The Holocaust was an obscene period in our nation's history. I mean in this century's history. But we all lived in this century. I didn't live in this century.' – Dan Quayle, former US Vice President

'Half the lies our opponents tell about us are not true.' – Sir Boyle Roche MP

'John Redwood is a young man, but let's face it, so was Margaret Thatcher in the 1970s.' – Edward Leigh MP

'I will never forget the '81 – or was it the '82? – honours list.' – Julian Critchley MP

'I love sports. Whenever I can, I always watch the Detroit Tigers play baseball on the radio.' – President General Ford

'We are not wholly an island. Except geographically.' – Prime Minister John Major

'Headmasters tend to be men.' – Clare Short MP

'China is a big country, inhabited by many Chinese.' – French president Charles de Gaulle

'If crime went down one hundred per cent, it would still be 50 times higher than it should be.' – John Bowman, Washington DC Councilman

'I told you to make one longer than the other, and instead you've made one shorter than the other – the opposite.' – Sir Boyle Roche MP

Chapter 11

LIVING IN A STATISTICAL WORLD

1 inch (2.5cm) – that's how much taller women are now than they were 50 years ago.

2.6 calories are burned during a single kiss.

4 is the number of aardvarks in the UK – two at Colchester Zoo and two at Suffolk wildlife park.

6 months – the average time a shopper spends in supermarkets in a lifetime... and the average woman gets through 6lb (2.7kg) of lipstick

13 per cent of UK women claim to know within ten minutes of meeting a man whether or not they will sleep with him.

18 per cent of men have paid for sex – but fewer than one per cent of women.

19 minutes is the average time spent preparing a meal in a British home.

20 – the number of pieces of chewing gum per square metre of pavement in the London borough of Westminster.

35 per cent of men and 14 per cent of women admit to having 'one last fling' on their stag or hen night. Of those women, 72 per cent go on to call off the wedding.

£35.29 is the average that a woman spends on new clothes for a date, plus £15.24 on beauty products.

37 people went to casualty last year with injuries involving tea cosies. Another 185 were hurt by bottle openers and 14,149 by vegetables.

37 people have been killed in Britain since 1978 while trying to shake items out of vending machines.

39.3 years is the age of the average Briton.

49 per cent of UK women own a sex toy – and 52 per cent of female Icelanders use them to keep warm.

54 is the average age of UK grandparents.

61 per cent of men prefer lager to any other drink.

70 per cent of people are cremated when they die.

36C is the average UK bra size. That's up from 34B ten years ago.

140 pints (80 litres) of water are used in the average bath, but a shower uses only 61.5 pints (35 litres).

81 years is the average life expectancy for British women – for men it is only 77.

97 per cent of all dangerous driving offences are committed by men.

156 mph (251km/h) is how fast an erotic sensation travels through our body from stimulated skin to the brain.

41 per cent of people spend more time in the bath than they do exercising.

£471 is the average weekly wage for a UK man. Women earn £372 on average.

850 Christmas cards are sent each year by the Queen and the Duke of Edinburgh.

1,869 patients had an abdominoplasty – that's the technical name for a tummy tuck – in the UK in 2005.

300 – the number of times the average person is picked up per day on one of the 2.5 million CCTV cameras in the UK.

4,393 UK nurses left to work in Australia and New Zealand in 2004.

10,000 – that's how many centenarians there were in the UK last year.

36,000 – the number of professional actors in the UK.

51,108 – the number of alcohol-related hospital admissions last year.

£3 million is the total cost of UK electricity bills for 13 per cent of Brits who leave their TVs on standby when they go on holiday.

4 million Brits will commit adultery this year.

6.3 million Brits have died from smoking in the past 50 years – nearly the population of London.

10.5 million is the UK cow population. Each one cow can produce 880 pints (500 litres) of methane gas a day.

171 million cookbooks are owned in Britain, but 61 million are never opened.

£280 million was spent on hair removal by British women last year.

£390 million worth of mobile phones are stolen each year in Britain – one every 12 seconds.

£1.46 billion a year is spent by Brits at car-boot sales.

4.7 billion sausages were eaten in Britain last year, along with 10 billion eggs – and 6 billion cups of tea were drunk.

£3.1 billion is the total amount we spend on chocolate every year.

4.6 billion bus journeys were made in Britain last year.

£6 billion is the amount spent by UK women on beauty products each year.

THE APPLIANCE OF SCIENCE

More and more young people are turning their backs on sciences at school in favour of 'softer' arts subjects like history and English. In fact, British industry chiefs recently warned of the damage this is doing to our economy because there just aren't enough people to take science jobs. But science can be fascinating and rewarding, as the following facts show.

BIOLOGY

The low frequency call of the humpback whale is the loudest noise made by a living creature. It is louder than Concorde and can be heard from 500 miles (804km) away.

The adult body has 206 bones – children are actually born with 300, but some of their bones fuse together as they get older.

If you spread the skin of one average human out flat it would cover nearly two-and-a-half square yards (2sq m).

The silkworm moth has eleven brains.

The housefly eats its food… then regurgitates it and eats it again.

Pound for pound, the femur – your thighbone – is stronger than reinforced concrete.

Maggots are good for you… Wounds infested with them heal quickly and without the spread of gangrene or other infection.

There are more living organisms on the skin of each human than there are humans on the surface of the Earth.

Men produce one thousand sperm cells each second – 86 million each day.

Human tapeworms can grow up to 75ft (22.9m) long.

At 15in (38cm), the eyes of giant squids are the largest on Earth.

You pick up more germs shaking hands than kissing.

Mosquitoes are attracted to the colour blue twice as much as to any other colour.

The average human heart beats more than 100,000 times a day.

Human birth control pills work on gorillas.

The octopus's testicles are in its head.

One in every 2,000 babies is born with a tooth.

CHEMISTRY

Sugar was first added to chewing gum in 1869 – by a dentist called William Semple.

Tomato ketchup was once sold as a medicine.

Gold and copper were the first metals to be discovered by man, in about 5000BC [small caps]. Together with silver they are found in their metallic state in the Earth's crust.

Magnesium was used in early flash photography because it burns with a brilliant light.

Airships used to be filled with hydrogen but now helium is used because they kept blowing up. One of the most famous was The Hindenburg, which exploded in 1937 in a huge fireball just 34 seconds after flames broke out.

Pearls melt in vinegar.

The hottest flame known is produced with carbon subnitride (C_4N_2) which can generate a temperature of 4,988°C (9,010°F).

Fizzy drinks became popular in 1832 after John Mathews invented an apparatus for getting the carbon dioxide gas into water.

Alcohol is added to soap to make it clear.

The oldest man-made alloy is bronze.

The chemical element carbon has the highest melting point of all the elements – so high that in our atmosphere it actually has no melting point.

Diamond is the hardest material known to man. The gem can be cut only by other diamonds. Even its name shows its strength. It comes from the ancient Greek 'adamas', meaning 'invincible'.

Soda water does not actually contain soda.

Thomas Edison is most commonly known as the inventor of the light bulb, but he also had some very silly ideas. He tried to invent a gunpowder-powered engine for a helicopter – but blew up his lab and decided to shelve the idea.

PHYSICS

Travelling at the speed of light, it would take a spaceship just 1.2822 seconds to reach the Moon.

But our current rockets would take 70,000 years to reach even the nearest star.

Somewhere in the flicker of a badly tuned TV set is the background radiation from the Big Bang.

The deepest part of any ocean is the Mariana Trench in the Pacific, with a depth of 35,797ft (10,900m).

The noise a whip makes when it is cracked is the result of a mini sonic boom.

Many people think that the nearest planet to Earth is Mars – but it's actually Venus.

Astronauts train in swimming pools in their spacesuits to simulate spacewalks.

Spacesuits weigh up to 440lb (200kg). After two or three hours' work underwater, even the fittest astronaut loses nearly 9lb (4kg) in body weight.

Lightening occurs about 100 times every second around the world – but only 25 of these strike the ground.

The planet Earth is around 4.56 billion years old – and man has existed only for 0.1 per cent of its history.

Light travels almost 1 million times faster than sound.

Even if we could travel at the speed of light – 186,000 miles (299,337km) a second – it would take 2 million years for us to reach Andromeda, the nearest large galaxy to us.

The universe contains more than 100 billion galaxies.

If the Sun were the size of a beach ball then Jupiter would be the size of a golf ball and the Earth would be as small as a pea.

The temperature at the centre of the Earth is estimated to be 5,500°C (9,932°F).

Sir Isaac Newton was just 23 years old when he devised the law of gravity.

Chapter 12

BABY LOVE

Are babies more than just vomiting, gurgling nuisances that keep you up all night? Even at your most sleep-deprived, you'd be hard-pressed not to marvel at some of the amazing facts about little ones!

Children born in May are on average 7oz (200g) heavier at birth than children born in any other month.

A child does not grow while it has a common cold.

The average toddler takes 176 steps a minute.

Six-year-olds laugh an average of 300 times a day. Adults only laugh around 60 times a day.

Up until the age of six or seven months, a child can breathe and swallow at the same time. Adults cannot.

Babies are born with the ability to swim and hold their breath, but they quickly lose this instinct.

Babies have nice-smelling breath because they have no teeth – teeth collect bacteria, which make our breath smell.

A newborn baby's head makes up about a quarter of its entire weight.

Most babies recognise their mothers' voices when they are born, but take around fourteen days to learn to recognise their father's voice.

Newborn babies are always born with blue eyes, but the colour can change within a few minutes of delivery.

Babies like pretty faces better than plain ones.

Young babies don't sweat because their sweat glands have not fully developed.

In toddlers, most choking accidents that don't involve food are caused by balloons (29 per cent) and balls and marbles (19 per cent).

A four-month-old foetus will turn away if a bright light is shone on the mother's belly. They also react to sudden loud noises.

When babies are born, parts of their skull overlap to help them squeeze out – leaving the head temporarily cone-shaped after delivery.

A human foetus acquires fingerprints at the age of three months.

A newborn baby focuses best at objects that are 10in (25cm) from the bridge of its nose – that's roughly the distance from its mother's breast to her eyes.

Babies don't have kneecaps when they are born. They only develop between six months to a year.

Babies like high-pitched singing voices.

About a quarter of all children go sleepwalking at least once between the ages of seven and twelve.

Children grow twice as fast in spring as they do in autumn, but they put on more weight in autumn than in spring.

Ultrasound scans often catch babies smiling. But the birth seems to ruin their good mood, as they rarely smile again for around a month after their birth.

Babies' strongest sense is smell and they can recognise their mothers by scent alone.

A baby is born somewhere in the world every three seconds.

Pound for pound, babies and toddlers are stronger than an ox, especially in their legs.

Babies learn sign language before they can talk. They learn the meaning of waving goodbye, hugging and kissing long before they can speak.

An embryo's heart begins to beat just three weeks after conception.

No matter when your baby is born, he or she will share a birthday with around 9 million other people.

One in five toddlers can open medicine bottles with child-resistant tops.

By the time of birth, a baby's brain is made up of more than 10 million nerve cells.

The record for the largest number of babies born to one woman is an eye-watering 69.

Playing classical music, especially Mozart, increases a baby's intelligence.

A boy's voice breaks during puberty because his vocal cords are lengthening. Up until that point, girls' and boys' vocal chords are the same size.

Most newborns cry without tears until they are three to six weeks old.

Eating fish during pregnancy can boost your baby's brain power, a study of 7,000 mothers found.

Will your baby be left or right-handed? It's decided as early as ten weeks in the womb, say researchers who found that babies use one hand more than the other – the same one they'll prefer to use after birth.

Men are officially the fastest at changing a baby. Research shows that the average time taken by a woman to change a baby is 2 minutes and 5 seconds – but the average man takes only 1 minute and 36 seconds.

A newborn baby will double its weight by six months and triple it by the end of the first year. If it carried on at that rate, it would weigh more than 1,000lb (4,535kg) by the time it was five.

Chapter 13

DON'T QUOTE ME – PLEASE!

Bungling George Bush put his foot in it big time when he mocked journalist Pete Wallsten for wearing sunglasses on a cloudy day… then found out the *Los Angeles Times* reporter was blind. Ouch! But plenty of other famous folk have made incredibly stupid remarks and done the dumbest things you could imagine.

'I've got ten new pairs of trainers – that's one for every day of the week.' – Topless model Sam Fox

'I'd rather be dead than singing 'Satisfaction' when I'm 45.' – Rolling Stone Mick Jagger, still singing it at… er…

'... And how long have you had this lifelong ambition?' – DJ Gary Davis

'Tony Blair is a complete dickhead.' – Spanish politician José Bono, unaware that his microphone was on and he could be heard on TV

'Ah, isn't that nice. The wife of the Cambridge president is kissing the cox of the Oxford crew.' – Harry Carpenter commentating on the boat race

'Every prime minister needs a Willie.' – Margaret Thatcher praising her deputy, William Whitelaw, in 1991

'I have already thanked the people of Liverpool for the honour of being a citizen of this famous city.' – Former South African president Nelson Mandela being given the freedom of Leeds in 2001

'Sales of the impotence drug Viagra will be subject to stiff restrictions.' – C5 News presenter

'Some of our earrings are cheaper than a Marks & Spencer prawn sandwich – but probably won't last as long. We also do cut-glass sherry decanters complete with six glasses on a silver-plated tray that your butler can serve you drinks on – all for £4.95. People say: "How can you sell this for such a low price?" I say: "Because it's total crap."' – Jewellery chain boss Gerald Ratner. His speech wiped an estimated £500 million from the value of the company.

'My position is that I want to make our position clear – the example of Germany is just one example, for example.' – John Prescott, but we've no idea what he was talking about

'I'm proud of George. He has learned a lot about ranching since that first year when he tried to milk a horse. A male horse.' – Laura Bush, America's First Lady on her husband George W. Bush

'People realise that although it could be you, it probably won't be. You'd be lucky to win a tenner.' – Lottery boss Dianne Thompson in 2002

'The bowler's Holding, the batsman's Willey.' – Cricket commentator Brian Johnston as England's Peter Willey faced Michael Holding of the West Indies.

'For those of you watching in black and white, Spurs are in the yellow strip.' – Commentator John Motson

'I've been up and down so many times that I feel as if I'm a revolving door.' – Actress and singer Cher

'It's not really about taking your clothes off.' – Actress Demi Moore on a film about strippers

'I was saying the other day, how often the most vulnerable area for goalies is between their legs.' – Andy Gray

'I'm the Hiroshima of love.' – Sylvester Stallone

'Very few of our customers have to wear suits to work. They'll be for his first interview or first court case.' – TopMan brand director David Shepherd explaining in 2001 that his male target customers were football hooligans

'I don't know all the certain words to it.' – Rap star Vanilla Ice on why his autobiography had a ghost writer

'Most are fairly stupid. I don't like many of them.' – 007 actor Timothy Dalton on women

'Hitler was a great leader.' – Kate Lawler on RI:SE TV

'There's nothing wrong with the car except it's on fire.'
'With the race half gone, there is half the race still to go.'
'He's obviously gone for a wheel change – I say 'obviously' because I can't see it.'
– Three gems from legendary motor-racing TV commentator, Murray Walker

'I couldn't settle in Italy. It was like living in a foreign country.' – Footballer Ian Rush on his move to Juventus

'The worst drug today is not smack or pot, it's refined sugar. Sugar kills!' – Actor George Hamilton

'God had to create disco music so that I could be born and be successful.' – Singer Donna Summer

'He speaks English, Spanish… and he's bilingual too.' – Boxing promoter Don King on boxer Julio Cesar Chavez

'If I had a choice of having a woman in my arms or shooting a bad guy on a horse, I'd take the horse. It's a lot more fun.' – Actor Kevin Costner

'All homosexuals should be castrated.' – Evangelist Billy Graham, a statement for which he later apologised

'I love rosé wine, but prefer the cheap stuff. When we go to posh restaurants, I always want to ask: "Got any Blossom Hill?"' – Coleen McLoughlin, fiancée of Wayne Rooney

'I can never get enough of the Tower Of London. It is just so ancient. The oldest thing we have in New York is the Starbucks on 79th Street.' – Actress Scarlett Johansson

'There is certainly more in the future now than back in 1964.' – Rock star Roger Daltrey of The Who

'Raquel, before I get into you, I must pause for this commercial.' – Interviewer David Frost to his chat show guest Raquel Welch

Chapter 14

COMPETITIVE SPORTS? ON SECOND THOUGHTS...

OK, so we made a dismal showing in the last World Cup, and are still a few years away from having another crack at the trophy. But don't worry. There are plenty more contests out there that we might become world champs in. How about Dwarf Tossing, Bog Snorkelling or Arm Farting?

Cheese Rolling

Don't go for a cheese roll in Brockworth, Gloucestershire – you could end up in hospital. Every May Bank Holiday, hundreds of competitors chase 7lb (3.1kg) rounds of cheese down a grass slope on a gradient that's 1 in 1 at some points.

International Rotten Sneaker Contest

Kids ranging from 5 to 15 compete all over the world from Alaska to Italy for a place in the grand final in Montpelier, Vermont, each March. The most stinky, worn-out, frayed and torn sneakers are enshrined in the Hall of Fumes.

Worm Charming

The world record for persuading earthworms to come to the surface in the tiny village of Willaston, near Nantwich, Cheshire, is 511 in half an hour, set in 1980.

Arm Farting

Don't knock it till you've tried it. This is one of the highlights of the annual Redneck Games, which is held once a year in East Dublin, Georgia, USA. It attracts crowds of more than 10,000. In the Arm Farting event, contestants have to play a tune by making that squelchy noise with their hand in their armpit. Other events include bobbing for pigs' feet, a mud-pit belly flop and killing bugs with spit balls. Most football players would probably be quite good at that one.

Dwarf Tossing

The first World Dwarf Tossing Championship was held in Australia in 1986 – and won by Great Britain's team of Danny Blue, Roy Merrin and Lenny the Giant. Dwarves in padded clothing are hurled onto mattresses. The world record is held by a man known as Cuddles, who tossed Lenny the Giant an impressive 12ft and 3in (1.9m).

Wife Carrying

You can win your Missus's weight in beer at the annual Wife Carrying Championships in Sonkajarvii, Finland. Thousands gather in July to watch men run 254m (833ft) over sand, grass, tarmac and through two water-filled ditches – with a wife on their back. It doesn't have to be your wife, either – any female over seventeen will do. Points are lost for dropping the poor woman.

World Sauna Championships

No sweat for this one. All contestants have to do is sit in a sauna for as long as possible. The temperature is 110°C (230°F), though, and half a litre (0.8 pints) of water is added to the hot coals every 30 seconds. They've been holding this championship in the Finnish town of Heinola since 1991 and just to make it tough, you have to keep your buttocks and thighs on the seat at all times, with forearms on your knees – and you can't wipe away any sweat.

World Gurning Championships

Having a face like Wayne Rooney or Gary Neville would be a head start in this contest, which is held every September at the Egremont Crab Fair in the Lake District. Competitors wear a leather horse collar and the winner is the one who gets most applause.

World's Biggest Liar

One winner claimed to have made a fortune mermaid farming. Each year in Wasdale, Cumbria, contestants in the Bridge Inn get two to five minutes to fib their way to victory.

Black Pudding Throwing

This apparently dates back to the Wars of the Roses. The World Championship is held in the village of Ramsbottom, where black puddings, famous in Lancashire, are tossed underarm at a stack of Yorkshire puddings. The winner is the one who knocks over the most Yorkshire puds.

Bog Snorkelling

All you have to do is complete two lengths of the 177ft (54m) Bog Trench wearing snorkel, flippers and optional wet suit, but without using any recognised swimming strokes. This bizarre contest takes place every August Bank Holiday Monday at the Waen Thydd peat bog in Britain's smallest town, Llanwrtyd Wells, in Wales.

Man vs Horse Marathon

This is just what it says – a man races against a horse and rider over 22 miles (35.4km) across roads, farm tracks, footpaths and open moorland. It's another winner from the wacky town of Llanwrtyd Wells (see Bog Snorkelling). This annual event is now in its 26th year, and amazingly a man once won. In June 2004, Huw Lobb became the first runner to beat the horse home.

Chess Boxing

They may go together like Lampard and scoring penalties, but there really are competitions that combine the two. Opponents square up in alternate rounds of boxing and chess. It's played only in Europe at the moment, but followers claim it's about to take America by storm.

Watermelon Seed Spitting

Can you spit a melon pip farther than the current world record of 68ft 9in (20.9m)? They try every year in Luling, Texas, but no one has bettered the effort in 1989 by local man Lee Wheells (and it's recognised by *Guinness World Records*). Contestants are docked points for spitting into the crowd and disqualified for using the wrong type of seeds. That gets judges spitting mad.

Wellie Whanging

It started in Yorkshire and contestants have to hurl a Wellington boot as far as possible from a standing or running start. There are international versions too – Gumboot Throwing in New Zealand and Boot Throwing in Finland. You never know, they might have their own World Cup one day.

Chapter 15

FOOD FOR THOUGHT

We're fascinated by food and can't seem to get enough of it – or enough TV shows about cooking. But did you know that most of us have seven or more jars of spices in our cupboards, but only use three of them regularly? Or that even food experts can't agree about whether or not we should wash fruit before eating it? There's a lot we don't know about the nation's favourite obsession.

In ancient China, mice were eaten and considered a great delicacy.

There is more alcohol in mouthwash than in wine.

The world's deadliest mushroom is the Death Cap, which contains five different poisons that can cause diarrhoea and vomiting, closely followed by damage to the kidneys and liver.

In the Middle Ages, chicken soup was thought to be an aphrodisiac.

Cheese is the oldest of all man-made foods.

Froth on beer will vanish if you lick your finger and then stick it in the beer.

The bat image on the Bacardi rum label is there because the soil where the sugar cane grows is fertile from the animals' guano (droppings).

Natural peanut oil is used for cooking in submarines because it doesn't smoke unless heated to immense temperatures.

If you chew gum while peeling onions, you will not cry.

Banana trees are not trees at all, but rhizomes.

Aubergines belong to the thistle family.

Turkey contains an amino acid called tryptophan, which causes sleepiness.

A wild but edible plant called hernandulcin is a thousand times sweeter than sugar.

The Egyptians ate mustard by throwing the seeds into their mouths as they chewed fresh meat.

Most of the vitamin C in fruit is found in the skins.

You can spin a hard-boiled egg, but not an uncooked or soft-boiled one.

Potatoes contain no fat at all, and the thicker the chip, the less fat it absorbs during cooking.

Ice cream was originally made without sugar or eggs.

The word 'whisky' comes from the Gaelic 'uisge beatha', meaning 'water of life'.

In ancient times, sprigs of parsley were thought to prevent drunkenness.

Bars of chocolate each contain an average of eight insects' legs.

Worcestershire sauce is basically an anchovy ketchup.

Paper can be made out of asparagus.

To make a pound of honey, bees have to visit 2 million flowers and fly the equivalent of twice around the world.

Tea bags were first launched in the 1920s.

Milk chocolate was first made by a man called Daniel Peter, who later sold his idea to his neighbour, Henri Nestlé.

In ancient Rome, it was considered a great sin to eat the skin of a woodpecker.

More than a third of all pineapples come from Hawaii.

The first ever recorded pizza parlour, Port Alba in Naples, opened in 1830 and is still open today.

Roughly 27 per cent of all the food produced in developed countries each year is thrown away.

In medieval England, breakfast was often served with beer.

Chocolate was used as a medicine in the 18th century.

The turnip originated in Greece.

Grapes explode if you cook them in a microwave.

In beer commercials, liquid detergent is often added to the glasses to make the drink foam more than usual.

Grasshoppers are the most popular insect snack in some parts of the world.

Bubbles in Guinness sink to the bottom of the glass rather than float to the top like all other beers.

Most alcoholic drinks contain the thirteen key minerals that are needed to sustain human life.

Apples, potatoes and onions all have the same taste and their apparently different flavours come from their smell.

There are more than 15,000 different types of rice.

Sixty cows can produce a ton (1,016kg) of milk a day.

Corn is the only cereal crop that has American origins.

In its natural state, the cashew nut contains a poisonous oil. Roasting destroys the oil and makes the nut safe to eat.

The term 'poached' for eggs actually means 'eggs in a bag', from the French word *poche*.

The Romans used poisonous lead as a food sweetener.

One in five chickens in our supermarkets is infected with Campylobacter, a bacterium that can cause food poisoning.

If you attach a battery to a pickle with wires, it will glow.

In the Middle Ages, sugar was treasured as a luxury and cost nine times more than milk.

There are more than 200 types of chilli peppers, but not one belongs to the pepper family.

China produces more apples than the rest of the world put together.

The average French person eats about 500 snails a year.

In early Roman times, flamingo tongues were pickled and served as a delicacy. Later, miners in the Andes of South America killed the birds for their fat, believing it to be a cure for tuberculosis.

Chapter 16

YOU'RE NOT FROM ROUND HERE, THEN?

Have thee got a face that'd frick'n a police horse? Are you in doubles or, have ya gorra bag on? Visitors to the UK may think we all speak the Queen's English, but regional dialects like Geordie, Scouse, Tyke or Yam-Yam, can sound like foreign languages. Tourist bosses in Wigan have even produced mugs and T-shirts with the local lingo and translations.

MANC (MANCHESTER)

Aright, our kid. Are you sorted?
– Hello, mate. Are you OK?

I gotta chip… it's my bath time.
– It's time to go.

I've had too much scoop an' I'm off the dials.
– I'm drunk.

Me 'ead's cabbaged.
– I'm confused.

What are ya skenning at?
– What are you looking at?

That scrote was bang out of order an' he's lucky the Dibble weren't here.
– That yob did something bad and he's lucky there were no police around.

WIGAN-ESE

As't feckl't it?
– Have you fixed it?

He's a reight blethereyed.
– He's not very bright.

Her's gerrin agate er mi.
– She is getting on at me.

Ah wur fair klempt.
– I was starving.

Am powfagged un jigger't.
– I am totally exhausted.

Her'd frick'n a police horse.
– She's not very good looking.

SCOUSE (LIVERPOOL)

Iz tart's dahr'ugly, sheed frighten a sailor off I a raft.
– His girlfriend is very ugly.

Ders more fat onna chip dan imm.
– He's very skinny.

She's goran arse like two dinner cobs in a docker's hankie.
– She has a big bum.

Hold me chips, Maggie, I'm took.
– Yes, I would like to dance.

EAST MIDLANDS

Aya gorra weeya?
– Is the wife with you?

Ee's gorra reet bag on.
– He's in a terrible mood.

Warra load of rammel!
– What a load of old rubbish!

Yaw wer laropped, Old Cock.
– You were very drunk, pal.

Who's mashing?
– Who's making the tea?

NORFOLK

I got suffen a-shew yo.
– I have something to show you.

Um nowagorn.
– I'm going now.

Tha's a lotta ol squit.
– That's a lot of nonsense.

Um hoolly dry.
– I'm very thirsty.

GLASWEGIAN

Dae ye think ma heid buttons up the bac'?
– Do I look stupid?

Nae-borra.
– Don't worry.

Gerr up the weansgreetin.
– Get the baby. He's crying.

Maheidsburstin.
– I've a hangover.

Geeascheeperhen. Yerasmasher.
– Give us a kiss, love. You're fit.

RADNORSHIRE (WALES)

He was in doubles.
– He was shaking with laughter.

I went to church and fetched the burying after.
– I went to the funeral and then on to the graveside.

He's made me mad and I'm going to call him over.
– He's infuriated me and I shall give him a dressing down.

YAM YAM (BLACK COUNTRY)

He's copped the fork wi me.
– He's taken umbrage.

She's gettin' on me pip with er larkin around and I'm gettin' on a line.
– She is getting on my nerves with her stupid behaviour and I am about to lose my temper.

Shut yer gob, there's a buzz comin.
–You have got a mouth that's big enough to swallow a bus.

We am on we olidaze.
– We are on holiday.

Yer want coal crackin' on yer 'ead, lad!
– You are a stupid boy!

SOMERSET

Ow beyon, meeyole muckers?
– How are you, my old friends?

She'm got half a yard of pump water.
– She has very straight hair.

You'm spack and spry but I can't happer on, I must stiver on.
– You're lively but I can't stop and chat, I must get going.

It'll be mags diversions when the others get wind.
– There'll be a row when the others find out.

BRUMMIE (BIRMINGHAM)

Put kettle on, orkid, I got a gob full a fevers.
– Make me a cup of tea, love, I'm parched.

He's got a bob on hisself.
– He thinks a lot of himself.

It's black uvva Bill's Muvva's.
– There's a storm on the way.

GEORDIE (NEWCASTLE)

Ye knaa what ah mean, leik?
– Do you know what I mean?

Eeeh man, ahm gannin te the booza.
– I'm off to the pub.

Whees in the netty?
– Who's in the loo?

Div aa knaa him? Ah divvint.
– Do you know him? I don't.

Gan canny or we'll dunsh sum-mick!
– Careful or we'll crash!

Ye mevvies misdoot me.
– I don't think you trust me.

TYKE (YORKSHIRE)

Put t'wood in t'ole!
– Shut the door!

Ees proper shuck!
– He's crazy!

She's nobbut just got the 'ippins off 'er backside and she's tin'.
– She's barely out of nappies and she's got a boyfriend.

Th'arl come to thi cake an' milk.
–You'll get what's coming to you.

DEVON

An appledrain stinged me on the neddick.
– A wasp stung me on the neck.

Uz bay gwain to Bareum on charabang safanoon.
– We're going to Barnstaple on the bus this afternoon.

Ow be fairin, maid? Yur in a proper jakes.
– How are you doing, young lady? You're in a right state.

Owbe nackin vore, my luvver?
– How are you doing, my dear?

The buyz gon perp.
– The lad's sulking.

He'm gone in like a baked dinner.
– He's drunk.

COCKNEY (LONDON)

What beautiful minces.
– You have nice yes.

Will you pass the army?
– Can I have the gravy?

I've got a new uncle but I need to get me weasel cleaned.
– I bought a new shirt but I should get my coat cleaned.

Take the apples and tell the trouble she's wanted on the dog.
– Go upstairs and tell my wife there is a phone call for her.

Chapter 17

FLIGHTS OF FANCY

Have you ever realised just how plane stupid people can be? Millions of Brits will go abroad this summer and you do get some daft ones. Some will ask for the windows to be opened – and the air crew can have attitude at altitude, too. Read on and you'll be too busy laughing to be afraid of flying.

Pilot: 'Ladies and gentlemen, this is your captain. The weather is good and we should have a smooth and uneventful flight. Oh my God…'
Pilot (five minutes later): 'Ladies and Gentlemen, I am sorry if I scared you earlier. While I was talking, the flight attendant spilled hot coffee in my lap. You should see the front of my pants.'
Passenger: 'That's nothing. Just see the back of mine.'

Pilot: 'Welcome to this Delta Airlines flight. We have some of the industry's best flight attendants. Unfortunately, none of them are on this flight.'

Air traffic controller: 'United 329, you have traffic – a Fokker at one o'clock, three miles, Eastbound.'
Pilot: 'Approach, I've always wanted to say this: I've got the little Fokker in sight.'

Air stewardess: 'As you exit the plane, please make sure to gather all of your belongings. Anything left behind will be distributed evenly among the flight attendants. Please do not leave spouses or children.'

Passenger: 'Do the pilots know about the aircraft that is flying very close to us?'
Air stewardess: 'Madam, that is just the light on the wing tip.'

Passenger: 'Can I sit next to the emergency exit?'
Air steward: 'No problem.'
Passenger: 'Will it be draughty by the door?'
Air steward: 'No madam, but if it starts to make a hissing noise, please let me know.'

Air traffic controller: 'US Air 2771, where the hell are you going? I told you to turn right on to Charlie taxiway. You turned right on Delta. Stop right there. I know it's difficult for you to tell the difference between C and D, but get it right. God. Now you've screwed everything up! It'll take forever to sort this out. You stay right there and don't move till I tell you to. You can expect progressive instructions in about half an hour and I want you to go exactly where I tell you, when I tell you, and how I tell you. You got that?'
Pilot: 'Wasn't I married to you once?'

Stewardess: 'Please remain seated as Captain Kangaroo bounces us to the terminal.'

Air stewardess: 'Ladies and gentlemen, please remain in your seats until Captain Crash and the crew have brought the aircraft to a screeching halt against the gate. And, once the tyre smoke has cleared and the warning bells are silenced, we'll open the door and let you pick your way through the wreckage to the terminal.'

Air steward: 'That was quite a bump, and I know what you all are thinking. I'm here to tell you it wasn't the airline's fault, it wasn't the pilot's fault, and it wasn't the flight attendant's fault. It was the asphalt.'

Pilot: 'Ladies and gentlemen, we've reached cruising altitude. In the event of a sudden loss of cabin pressure, masks will descend from the ceiling. Stop screaming, grab the mask, and pull it over your face. If you have a small child travelling with you, secure your mask before assisting with theirs. If you are travelling with more than one small child, pick your favourite.'

Pilot: 'We have now reached our cruising altitude, so I'll switch the seatbelt signs off. Feel free to move about as you wish but please stay inside the plane until we land. It's cold outside and if you walk on the wings it affects the flight pattern.'

Air steward: 'We'd like to thank you folks for flying with us today. And, the next time you get the insane urge to go blasting through the skies in a pressurised metal tube, we hope you'll think of US Airways.'

Passenger: 'Is it correct that it is minus 50 degrees outside?'
Air stewardess: 'Yes, that's correct. It's minus 50 degrees outside the aircraft.'
Passenger: 'You mean minus 50 degrees cold?'
Air stewardess: 'That's correct.'
Passenger: 'Then how come we're not all dead yet?'

Air stewardess: 'To operate your seat belt, insert the metal tab into the buckle and pull tight. It works just like every other seat belt and if you don't know how to operate one you probably shouldn't be out in public unsupervised.'

'We have a smoking section. Just ask and you will be escorted to the wing of the plane.'

'This window must be faulty... my daughter can't get it open.'

Air stewardess: 'We hope you enjoyed choosing us as much as we liked taking you for a ride.'

Chapter 18

YOU MAY TURN YOUR PAPERS OVER NOW

GCSE pass rates shot up to a record 98.1 per cent in 2006. But some critics claim that the exams have become too easy, and the government has promised that English and Maths GCSEs are to be made tougher. Even now not every candidate knows all the answers, though – and sometimes they get them very, very wrong.

HISTORY

The inhabitants of Egypt were called mummies. They lived in the Sarah Dessert and travelled by Camelot.

Sir Francis Drake circumcised the world with a 100ft clipper.

Queen Elizabeth exposed herself before her troops, and they all shouted 'Hurrah'. Then her navy defeated the Spanish Armadillo.

The sun never set on the British Empire 'cos it was in the east and sun sets in the west.

Nero was a cruel tyrant who would torture his poor subjects by playing the fiddle to them.

Gravity was invented by Issac Walton. It is chiefly noticeable in the autumn, when the apples are falling off the trees.

The nineteenth century was a time when people stopped reproducing by hand and started reproducing by machine.

History calls people Romans because the never stayed in one place for very long.

Solomon had more than 300 wives and 700 porcupines.

GEOGRAPHY

Q: Name the four seasons.
A: Salt, pepper, mustard and vinegar.

Q: What causes the tides in the oceans?
A: The tides are a fight between the Earth and the Moon. All water tends to flow towards the Moon, because there is no water on the Moon, and nature abhors a vacuum. I forget where the Sun joins in this fight.

Q: How is dew formed?
A: The Sun shines on leaves and makes them perspire.

Q: Explain one of the processes by which water can be made safe to drink.
A: Flirtation makes water safe to drink because it removes large pollutants like grit, sand, dead sheep and canoeists.

Q: What is a planet?
A: A body of earth surrounded by sky.

The Moon is planet just like the Earth only deader.

The chief animals of Australia are the kangaroo, larkspur, boomerang and peccadillo.

In Athens there is a temple called the Pancreas.

SOCIOLOGY

Q: What guarantees may a mortgage company insist on from a customer?
A: If you are buying a house, they will insist that you are well endowed.

Q: In a democratic society, how important are elections?
A: Very important. Sex can only happen when a male gets an election.

ENGLISH

Q: Use the word judicious in a sentence to show that you understand its meaning.
A: Hands that judicious can be soft as your face.

Q: What does the word benign mean?
A: Benign is what you will be after you be eight.

Q: What is a turbine?
A: Something a Sikh wears.

SCIENCE

Q: How are the main parts of the body categorised (e.g. abdomen)?
A: The body is consisted into three parts – the brainium, the borax and the abdominal cavity. The brainium contains the brain, the borax contains the heart and lungs, and the abdominal cavity contains the five bowels, A, E, I, O and U.

Q: Name a major disease that is associated with cigarettes.
A: Premature death.

Q: How can you delay milk from turning sour?
A: Keep it in the cow.

Q: What happens to a boy when he reaches puberty?
A: He says goodbye to his boyhood and looks forward to his adultery.

Q: What happens to your body as you age?
A: When you get old, so do your bowels and you get intercontinental.

Q: What is artificial insemination?
A: When the farmer does it to the bull instead of the cow.

Q: Give an example of a fungus. What is a characteristic feature?
A: Mushrooms. They always grow in damp places and that is why they look like umbrellas.

Q: What is the Fibula?
A: A small lie.

Q: What does varicose mean?
A: Nearby.

Q: Give the meaning of the term 'Caesarean Section'.
A: The Caesarean Section is a district in Rome.

Q: What is the most common birth control?
A: Most people have contraception by wearing condominium.

Q: What is a seizure?
A: A Roman emperor.

Q: What is a terminal illness?
A: Being sick at an airport.

The dodo is a bird that is almost decent by now.

The hookworm larvae enters the human body through the soul.

A magnet is something you find crawling all over a dead cat.

English sparrows and starlings eat the farmer's grain and his corpse.

The Earth makes one resolution every 24 hours.

The cuckoo bird does not lay his own eggs.

Geometry teaches us how to bisex angles.

Chapter 19

WEATHERING THE WEATHER

Brits know that the weather is more likely to be barmy than balmy, but things may be about to get worse. Scientists from Newcastle University recently predicted we're set to become monsoon UK with the kind of downpours that hit India and the tropics becoming typical during our autumns. More heatwaves are also on the way.

Hot weather is a killer. When New York was hit by a heatwave in 1988, temperatures reached 32°C (94°F) for 32 days and the murder rate shot up by 75 per cent.

Lightening kills about 10 per cent of its victims, mainly from heart attacks. That's about five people a year in the UK.

Snow exists on the equator on three mountains... Mount Kenya (17,057ft; 5,199m high) in Kenya, Mount Kilimanjaro (19,340ft; 5,895m) in Tanzania and Cotopaxi (20,702ft; 6,310m) in Ecuador.

Tornadoes rotate anti-clockwise in the northern hemisphere and clockwise in the southern hemisphere.

A lightening bolt travels at about 14,000mph (22,500km/h), bringing 300,000 volts of electricity to the ground in milliseconds. This heats the surrounding air to around 30,000°C (54,000°F) – five times hotter than the surface of the Sun.

On 10 June 1752, inventor Benjamin Franklin narrowly missed electrocuting himself while flying a kite with a key attached to it in a thunderstorm. His experiment showed lightning is a form of electricity and he went on to invent the lightning conductor.

The most intense downpour ever recorded was on the Caribbean Island of Guadeloupe, where 1.5in (38mm) of rain fell in just one minute.

The heaviest hailstones on record weighed more than 2lb (1kg) each and killed 92 people in Gopalganj,

Bangladesh on 14 April 1986. The biggest in the UK weighed 5oz (142g) and fell at Horsham in West Sussex in 1958.

London had zero hours of sun in December 1890.

It's only ever snowed once in Miami – in January 1977.

We earthlings have it easy – there's some wild weather elsewhere in our solar system. On Mars there are storms FOUR times the size of Texas. And Jupiter has a hurricane twice the size of our entire planet that's lasted for at least 300 YEARS.

If there is no wind, raindrops will fall at 7–18mph (3–8m per second). And if they travel any faster than 18 miles per hour, they break up because of air friction.

Raindrops aren't actually teardrop-shaped, as most weather maps show them, but spherical.

According to the Met Office, you have a 1 in 3 million chance of being zapped by lightning – higher than your chances of winning the Lotto jackpot, which is 1 in 14 million.

They say lightning never strikes twice, but Virginia park ranger Roy Sullivan was hit seven times between 1942 and 1977, according to *Guinness World Records*, and he survived them all.

Tree crickets are called the Poor Man's Thermometer – just count the number of chirps a cricket makes in 15 seconds, then add 37. The sum gives the temperature in Fahrenheit.

All the fossil fuel used by humans since the start of civilisation is equivalent to less energy than 30 days of sunshine.

The amount of sunlight reaching the Earth's surface is 6,000 times the amount of energy used by all human beings worldwide.

Tororo in Uganda has the most thunderstorms worldwide with an average of 251 days annually – that's 69 per cent of the year.

Warmer weather means more cases of food poisoning. They rise by 5 per cent for each one degree Celsius the temperature goes up – that's an extra 4,000 cases per degree in the UK.

How far away is a thunderstorm? Count the number of seconds between when you see the lightning and hear the thunder. Divide by two, and that's how many miles away the storm is.

A one degree Celsius increase in average temperature for a UK winter would save about 7,000 deaths from cold a year.

Floods kill more people worldwide each year than tornadoes, hurricanes or lightning.

There are a million avalanches worldwide every year, and they kill 150 people, who suffocate within minutes of being buried.

DRIEST

It would take an entire century to fill up a coffee cup in Arica, Chile – it gets only 0.03in (0.76mm) of rainfall every year.

WINDIEST

The windiest place on earth is Mount Washington in New Hampshire, USA. On 12 April 1934, a surface wind of 231mph (371km/h) was recorded there – quicker than most F1 cars.

COLDEST

The world's coldest recorded temperature was at the Vostok Scientific Station in Antarctica on 21 July 1983 – minus 89.6°C (-130°F).

HOTTEST

The highest temperature ever recorded in the world was a bone-boiling 58°C (136°F) at Al Aziziyah, Libya on 13 September 1922.

The hottest temperature measured in the UK was a sizzling 38.5°C (101F) in Brogdale, Kent in 2003. The coldest was minus 27.2°C (-17°F) in Braemar, Grampian in 1895 and 1982.

WETTEST

Himalayan village Mawsynram officially has the most rainfall in the world, with a drenching 450in (1,143cm) falling there every year.

Chapter 20

IT'S THE LAW, YOU KNOW...

Stick a stamp with the Queen's head on it upside down on a letter and you are committing treason. This law was passed in 1840, when the first Penny Black was issued, to stop people 'insulting the monarchy'.

It has been illegal to have sex on a parked motorcycle in London since a law passed just after World War Two.

A woman is allowed to bite off a man's nose if he kisses her against her will, in a law that dates back to 1837.

Munch on a mince pie this Christmas and you are breaking the law. Oliver Cromwell banned them in the seventeenth century because he said they were not Puritan enough.

All Englishmen over the age of fourteen must spend two hours a week practising the longbow, supervised by the local clergy. This law dates from the Middle Ages when there was no standing army, so in times of war noblemen were required to provide knights, archers and infantry.

Break your boiled egg at the pointed end and you can be put in the stocks for 24 hours under a law passed in 1561 by King Edward VI.

Wear a tall hat at the theatre and you could be fined, since someone sat in front of Oliver Cromwell and obstructed his view of the stage.

Don't make fun of a boxer during a bout or you're breaking the law and can be thrown into the street. 'Insulting or abusive remarks directed at the contestants' are out.

Be careful where you scatter a loved one's ashes, as you will be breaking the law if you spread them where they could contaminate the water supply.

Ever been lost going round a strange roundabout for the first time? Well, if you circle it more than three times, you could be arrested, as it is an offence.

No matter how heated Prime Minister's Question Time gets, Gordon Brown and David Cameron are banned from putting on armour in Parliament since a law passed in 1313.

Let a desperate stranger into your house to use the loo and – if you live in Scotland – you're committing an offence, according to a law dating from 1791.

Stealing post from the Royal Mail is an offence because it is still classed as an act of treason.

Couples in Birmingham can be fined £25 if they have sex 'on the steps of any church after the sun goes down'. However, the law says nothing about doing it in broad daylight.

A bloodhound is the only animal in the world whose evidence is admissible in a court of law.

It is illegal to take a cow along a road between the hours of 10am and 7pm – unless you have permission in advance from the Commissioner of Police.

Offer your local Father Ted a cup of tea and you can be tortured or even hanged under a law dating from Elizabeth I's reign that forbids 'harbouring a Catholic priest'.

Don't go to a fancy dress party as a Chelsea Pensioner. Because they are entitled to increased state benefits and subsidised housing, it is an offence to pretend you are one.

Men caught short in the street are legally allowed to urinate in public, but only on the rear wheel of their own car on the driver's side of the vehicle.

Spring cleaning? Hang a bed out of your window and you can be jailed for up to five years.

It is against the law to be drunk in a pub or bar says the Licensing Act, passed during World War One.

It is illegal to show affection in public in Wales on Sundays.

All cyclists must ring their bells non-stop while the bike is moving, says a law passed in 1888.

Hunks in Birmingham face a fine if they go topless in the city centre.

Riding a bike or a horse while drunk is illegal.

Boys under ten are forbidden to look at naked mannequins. This law dates from the reign of George V in the 1900s, when mannequins first began to appear in shop windows and young boys' eyes started popping out.

LOONY LAWS ARE NOT JUST RESTRICTED TO THE UK

Anyone who detonates a nuclear device in the city limits in Chico, California, can be fined $500 (about £260). If anyone's still around to collect it, that is.

Donald Duck comics were once banned in Finland because he never wore trousers.

Doctors are banned from looking directly at a woman's private parts in Bahrain, so docs who need to carry out examinations have to use a mirror.

It is illegal to set a mousetrap in California if you don't have a hunting licence.

The entire *Encyclopaedia Britannica* is banned in Texas because it contains a formula for making beer at home.

Men who wear skirts in Italy can be thrown in jail.

You can be thrown in jail in Myanmar for going on the Internet. Anyone found in possession of a modem can be imprisoned.

It is illegal for a man with a moustache to kiss a woman in Eureka, Nevada.

If a child burps in church in Nebraska, his or her parents can be arrested. It is also illegal in that state for a mother to give her daughter a perm without a licence.

Mickey Mouse was banned in Romania in 1935 because officials thought the sight of a 10ft-high (3m) rodent on screen would terrify the nation's children.

Chapter 21

WHY DO WE SAY THAT?

English has hundreds of everyday phrases. Everyone knows exactly what they mean, but where do they come from?

Close, but no cigar

Meaning: Come disappointingly close to success.

In the nineteenth century, Havana cigars were given away as prizes at fairs for sideshow games like shooting spots off a playing card or ringing a bell with a mallet. If you almost won, you were close… but didn't get the cigar.

Close your eyes and think of England

Meaning: To tolerate unwanted sex.

The phrase became popular in 1912 after the journal

of posh Lady Hillingdon was published. She wrote: 'I am happy now that Charles calls on my bed chamber less frequently than of old. As it is, I now endure but two calls a week and when I hear his steps outside my door I lie down on my bed, close my eyes, open my legs and think of England.'

Sweet Fanny Adams

Meaning: Nothing.

Fanny Adams was murdered in 1867 and her body horribly dismembered. Sailors in the British Navy used the expression for unpleasant-looking meals they were served but it later came to mean nothing of value.

Gordon Bennett!

Meaning: Exclamation of shock.

The original James Gordon Bennett II (1841–1918) was a colourful character. One of his many exploits saw him fly a plane through an open barn. The surprised onlookers were supposed to have said: 'That was Gordon Bennett!' which led to the shortened phrase.

Warts and all

Meaning: Leaving nothing unpleasant out.

When Oliver Cromwell was Lord Protector of England in the mid-seventeenth century, he commissioned artist Sir Peter Lely to paint his portrait, saying: 'I desire you would use all your skill to paint my picture truly like I am and not flatter me at all. Remark all these roughness, pimples, warts and everything as you see me.'

Smart Alec

Meaning: Too clever for your own good.

In the 1840s, New York City con man Aleck Hoag got his wife to pose as a prostitute so the pair could rob her clients. If they were caught, they bribed police to escape. When Hoag tried to double-cross an officer – thinking he wouldn't dare to complain – the cop did and Hoag landed in jail.

Have a hunck

Meaning: To have an instinctive feeling about an outcome.

In America in the 1900s gamblers believed that rubbing the hump of a hunchback would bring good luck. In medieval times, hunchbacks were thought to be possessed by the Devil and to be able to see into the future.

Crocodile tears

Meaning: Fake tears.

Crocodiles often secrete a fluid from their eyes when they kill prey. It may look as if they are sad and weeping but in fact they are feeling very smug. And full.

Peg out

Meaning: Die.

From the scoring in card games such as Cribbage in which the score is kept on a peg-board and the game ends when the first person 'pegs out' – that is, reaches the end.

Spill the beans

Meaning: Divulge a secret.

When votes were cast in ancient Greece, everyone secretly put either a white bean (for yes) or a black bean (for no) into a bag. Votes had to be unanimous, so if the collector dropped the bag before the end of vote and one black bean was seen, the result was immediately known.

Dead ringer

Meaning: An exact duplicate.

In racing, a ringer is a fast horse switched for a slower one that looks the same to fool the bookies. It originated in the US at the end of the nineteenth century – 'dead' meant 'exact' at the time.

Above board

Meaning: Without any trickery.

From gambling. If card players keep their hands above the table, or board, they can be seen to be playing fairly.

Hobson's choice

Meaning: No choice at all.

Businessman Tobias Hobson ran a thriving carrier and horse rental service in Cambridge at the turn of the seventeenth century – but never gave his customers the chance to choose their own mount.

Flash in the pan

Meaning: Something that disappoints by being over too quickly.

Muskets used to have small pans to hold the gunpowder fuse. If it flared up without firing the gun, it was known as a flash in the pan.

Get off scot free

Meaning: Avoid paying, or get away with it.

Americans believe the phrase comes from Dred Scott, a black slave born in Virginia in 1799 who tried to win his freedom in a series of court cases in 1857. He failed but was later freed by his owners. However, 'scot' is also a Scandinavian word for tax and was used in Britain in the thirteenth century. So 'scot free' means 'tax free'.

Bunny boiler

Meaning: An obsessive and dangerous female, in pursuit of a lover who has spurned her.

In the 1987 film *Fatal Attraction*, a scorned Glenn Close obsessively pursues her ex lover, Michael Douglas. The phrase comes from the chilling scene where she boils Douglas's daughter's pet rabbit.

Big cheese

Meaning: The most important person.

Used in the USA about 1890, but came from the British Empire in India. The Urdu word for thing is *chiz*. The British brought home the expression 'the cheese' for the main or best thing and it crossed the Atlantic as 'the big cheese'.

All singing, all dancing

Meaning: With many attributes.

From posters advertising the 1929 film *Broadway Melody*, which proclaimed the film to be: 'All talking, all singing, all dancing'.

The full monty

Meaning: Complete, the whole thing.

Thought to come from Sir Montague Burton, a Sheffield tailor, in 1906. A complete three-piece suit – one with a waistcoat for a wedding etc – would be the Full Monty. But another possible explanation comes from World War II, when Field Marshall Montgomery insisted his troops eat a full English breakfast every day.

Stool pigeon

Meaning: A police informer.

Hunters used to use decoy pigeons fixed to posts or stools to lure their quarry. The term was later used to describe people who helped the police by luring criminals into police traps, then for anyone who helped the police by informing on others.

Bad hair day

Meaning: When your hair is unmanageable – or a day when everything seems to go wrong.

Came into popular use after the 1992 film *Buffy the Vampire Slayer*. Buffy says to one-armed vampire Amilyn: 'I'm fine but you're obviously having a bad hair day.'

Get the sack

Meaning: To be fired from a job.

When tradesmen owned their tools and were dismissed from their job, they took the tools home in a bag or sack.

Acid test

Meaning: A test you can be sure of.

In the nineteenth-century California Gold Rush, prospectors splashed a little acid on to a metal to see if it was gold. Base metals react with acid but gold does not.

Bee's knees

Meaning: The absolute best there is.

Bees carry pollen back to their hive in sacks on their legs, so a bee's knees are crammed with goodness. First used in April 1922 in the Ohio newspaper *The Newark Advocate* in America.

Chew the cud

Meaning: To chat, in a slow and aimless manner.

Cud is part-digested food that ruminant animals such as cows bring back into their mouths from their first stomach to chew at leisure, giving the impression that they are having a slow, gentle conversation.

Darling buds of May

Meaning: Fresh and new but about to reach maturity.

The phrase that gave its name to the early nineties hit TV comedy show starring David Jason and Catherine Zeta-Jones refers to the opening buds that point toward the warm summer season ahead and to the freshness and exuberance of youth as it turns toward adult maturity.

Elvis has left the building

Meaning: The show is over.

First used in December 1956 by Horace Logan, the announcer at the Louisiana Hayride show where Elvis was a rising star. It was picked up and used at concerts by other singers to tell fans there would be no more encores.

Famous for fifteen minutes

Meaning: To have a moment of fame and then be forgotten.

Coined by sixties artist Andy Warhol in February 1968, when he predicted: 'In the future everybody will be world famous for fifteen minutes.' With the growth of reality shows like *Big Brother*, it seems to be coming true. How many housemates do you remember?

Go berserk

Meaning: Behave in a frenzied, violent way.

A Berserker was a Viking warrior who fought with wild ferocity. The name is thought to come from the 'bear sark' (meaning 'bear skin') that they wore.

Hit the ground running

Meaning: Get off to a quick start.

Soldiers having to land by parachute and go straight into action need to hit the ground running.

In the bag

Meaning: Good as sorted.

In Parliament, petitions were put in a bag under the Speaker's chair. Any in the bag would be debated that day.

Jerry built

Meaning: Built in a sloppy way to make a quick profit. First used in 1869 after the biblical city of Jericho which fell down when Joshua and the Israelites marched around it banging drums.

Kick the bucket

Meaning: To die.

The wooden frame that slaughtered animals were hung on is called a 'bucket', and death spasms of the animals made them seem to kick it.

Let the cat out of the bag

Meaning: To give away a secret.

A favourite trick at country markets used to be to sell a customer a costly pig but then actually give him a cheap cat that you had switched into the bag instead to cheat him. If someone let the cat out of the bag before you had time to vanish, the swindle was revealed.

Mum's the word

Meaning: Keep quiet – say nothing.

This does not come from mum as in 'mother', but from the humming sound. It was used by Shakespeare in *Henry VI Part 2*: 'Seal up your lips and give no words but mum'. Mummers were also well-known as medieval mime actors – and therefore silent.

No holds barred

Meaning: Without restrictions or rules.

This is a wrestling term dating from when there were no rules for fighting and therefore anything was allowed in the ring.

On a wing and prayer

Meaning: Just managing to get the job done.

From the World War II song: 'Coming in on a Wing and a Prayer' by Harold Adamson and Jimmie McHugh, written in 1943, about a damaged plane that just gets back to base.

Pipe down

Meaning: Be quiet.

On sailing ships, signals were given by blowing whistles or pipes. When an officer wanted a sailor sent below, he would have him 'piped down'.

Queer street

Meaning: Imaginary home for people in difficulty.

First recorded in 1811 in Grose's *Dictionary Of The Vulgar Tongue* as: 'Improper. Contrary to one's wish.'

Raining cats and dogs

Meaning: Raining very heavily.

In seventeenth-century England, city streets were filthy and heavy rain would wash dead animals along the gutters.

The bit between your teeth

Meaning: Take control.

When a horse bites on the bit it takes control from its rider.

Up a blind alley

Meaning: On the wrong track.

Alleys are blind if they have no exit at one end.

Veg out

Meaning: Relax mindlessly.

To behave like a vegetable by doing and thinking nothing. The phrase comes from the medical term of being in a persistent vegetative state in which severely brain-damaged patients are unable to move.

Whipping boy

Meaning: A scapegoat.

In the fifteenth-century English court, a Whipping Boy was beaten when the Crown Prince misbehaved.

X marks the spot

Meaning: Where something can be found.

From the seventeenth century, when sailors longed to find a pirate map with an X to show where treasure was buried.

You can lead a horse to water, but you can't make it drink

Meaning: You can only go so far unless others help.

Dates back to 1546 in John Heywood's book of English proverbs.

Zigzag

Meaning: Straight lines at angles.

In 1712, French gardener Jean-Baptiste Alexandre Le Blond spoke of: 'Steps of Grass laid in Zic-Zac.'

Chapter 22

HALLOWE'EN: SPOOKY SPIRITS AND THINGS THAT GO 'BUMP!' IN THE NIGHT

Witches, ghosts and ghouls roam the Earth every 31 October to scare us all to death on Hallowe'en. And if they don't get you, then trick or treat kids will do their best to behave like little monsters as well. But where did it all start, why is this night so spooky and where did all the superstitions come from?

Dead saints who don't have their own special day are remembered on 1 November – All Saints Day – with a mass called Allhallowsmass, and so the night before became known as All Hallows E'en or Hallowe'en.

To protect yourself on Hallowe'en, the Night of Enchantment, all journeys should be finished before sunset and you should carry a piece of bread crossed with salt in your pocket. The bread is holy and the salt used to repel witches

Pumpkins took over from turnips when Irish immigrants went to America and turnips were hard to find. They started using pumpkins for Hallowe'en lanterns instead and now the pumpkin has almost completely taken over.

Orange and black became Hallowe'en colours because orange is associated with harvests at the end of October and black with death.

Trick or treat was started in Victorian England to scare neighbours on Hallowe'en. Children would dress up as witches and ghosts to frighten people into giving them sweets and money. In those days, Hallowe'en was also known as Mischief Night.

These days trick or treating is normally a bit of harmless fun, but the tricks used to be more gruesome in the old days. In 1920s Britain, most toilets were outside and kids used to tip them over – even if someone was in them at the time.

Spiders on Hallowe'en are said to be the spirits of dead loved ones. If you see one on the night, they could be watching you.

The most haunted pub in England is the Ram Inn, Wotton-under-Edge, Gloucestershire. Two men who stayed the night there had such a fright they had to go and get a vicar to exorcise them. The vicar was so shocked he banned them from going back to the pub ever again.

Bonfires scare off evil spirits, according to ancient Celts, who believed that light had power over darkness. Some used to jump over bonfires to bring good luck.

Candlelight is said to scare witches away from your front door and stop them eating your children. This led to the tradition of putting candles in hollowed-out pumpkin lanterns on Hallowe'en.

The ancient Celts celebrated the festival of Samhain (meaning 'end of summer') at Hallowe'en when the year changed from light to dark. They feared the coming of winter because they thought spirits of the dead could then enter the world.

Black cats were originally believed to be a kind of cosmic sidekick for witches, protecting them from powers and forces that were hostile to them

Dressing up for Hallowe'en is meant to stop you being recognised by ghosts. People thought if they left their homes they would see demons, so they put on masks after dark hoping that ghosts would mistake them for fellow spirits.

The Romans brought their own festivals with them when they conquered Britain. They merged existing Celtic traditions like Samhain with their own important days, such as a harvest festival called Poloma, and a celebration for the dead called Feralia.

Jack-o'-lanterns were named after a man named Jack, who could not enter heaven when he died because he had been a miser. But he could not get into hell either, because he had played jokes on the Devil. So instead, he had to wander the Earth with his lantern until Judgement Day.

Spooky Hallowe'en cards were first put on sale in America in the 1920s and cost just a dime each.

Today, more than £50 million is spent on Hallowe'en greetings throughout the world.

Ghosts were kept away from people's houses on Hallowe'en by putting bowls of food outside front doors. People thought that the food would please the ghosts, stop their anger and make them less likely to haunt their homes.

Vampire bats do drink blood, but they don't come from Transylvania. They live in Central and South America and gorge themselves on cattle, horses and birds.

Sweet makers are big winners at Hallowe'en. It is estimated that £1.5 billion worth of sweets are sold worldwide for the night. It is by far the sweetest holiday of the year, beating Easter, Valentine's Day and even Christmas. One-quarter of all the sweets sold each year throughout the whole world are bought in the eight weeks from 15 September to 10 November.

Apple bobbing, or duck-apple, is a Roman game. People have been putting their heads in barrels full of water to find apples for more than 2,000 years. It began as a tribute to Pomona, the Roman goddess of fruit and trees.

The biggest pumpkin ever recorded being grown for Hallowe'en weighed a whopping 103st (654kg).

Pooky Night is Irish for Hallowe'en and is so called after the mischievous spirit Puca. In Welsh, it's Nos Calan Gaeaf.

Cucumbers are related to pumpkins because they are both from the squash family.

Girls used to put one hazelnut along the front of the fire grate to represent each of their suitors, then chant: 'If you love me, pop and fly. If you hate me, burn and die.' The fate of each nut revealed who the true lovers were.

Spalding in Lincolnshire claims to be the pumpkin capital of Britain, because it's the home of the country's biggest producer. David Bowman grows 2 million of them every year. ninety-nine per cent of all pumpkins sold are used as lanterns for Hallowe'en.

If you want to meet a witch on Hallowe'en, it's easy. Just put your clothes on inside out and walk backwards ten paces.

The fastest pumpkin carver in the world is Jerry Ayers, of Baltimore, Ohio. He has carved a pumpkin into a lantern in just 37 seconds.

Bell ringing is said to scare off evil spirits.

Peel an apple in one long strand and throw it over your shoulder. The shape it lands in will be the initial of your true love.

Lating or Lighting The Witches was a custom in Lancashire. People would carry candles from eleven to midnight. If the candles burned, the carriers were safe, but if the witches blew them out, the omens were bad.

Ancient Britons believed that winter was too cold for evil spirits, hobgoblins, imps and will-o'-the-wisps, who hid underground for six months from 1 November. So Hallowe'en was their last chance to play tricks on mortals.

HALLOWE'EN HUMOUR

What kind of streets do zombies live in?
Dead ends.

What do you get when you cross a vampire and a snowman?
Frostbite.

Why do witches fly on brooms?
Because vacuum cleaners are too heavy.

Chapter 23

OSCAR NIGHT

The frocks are fitted, the red carpet laid and the divas are decked out in the world's finest diamonds. Every year, the stars turn out in force for the Oscars ceremony. But how many of them know the following Tinseltown trivia?

The night's winners aren't revealed until the envelopes are opened. But the winners of the first Oscars were announced three months in advance.

Walt Disney won more Oscars than anyone else, with 26 to his name. He was nominated for 64.

Only 270 people attended the first awards ceremony, a banquet at the Blossom Room in the Hollywood Roosevelt Hotel in May 1929. Tickets cost just over £2.50 each.

The most awards won by a single film is eleven. Three films have done it – *Ben Hur*, *Titanic* and, most recently, *The Lord Of The Rings: The Return Of The King*.

The Return Of The King is the only film ever to have won every single Oscar it was nominated for.

German actor Emil Jannings won the first ever Best Actor award for his roles in *The Last Command* and *The Way Of All Flesh*.

Janet Gaynor was the first Best Actress for her role in three different films – *Sunrise*, *Seventh Heaven* and *Street Angel*.

In 2002, American TV presenter Jules Asner shimmied along the red carpet wearing a £2-million dress, believed to be the most expensive ever made. Designed by Anne Bowen, it was created using 5,000 specially cut diamonds.

The youngest person to win an honorary Oscar is Shirley Temple, who was just five when she got an award recognising her talent as a child star.

The youngest person to win a standard Oscar is Tatum O'Neal, who was ten when she won Best Supporting Actress for 1973's *Paper Moon.*

The oldest person to win an Oscar is Jessica Tandy, with Best Actress for *Driving Miss Daisy* in 1989, aged 80.

The actress with most Oscars is Katharine Hepburn, who was nominated twelve times and won four Best Actress Oscars for her roles in *Morning Glory*, *Guess Who's Coming To Dinner*, *Eleanor Of Aquitaine* and *On Golden Pond.*

Cedric Gibbons, the MGM art director, designed the famous statuettes and Los Angeles-based sculptor George Stanley brought the figure to life.

Accepting her Best Actress Oscar in 1943, Greer Garson gave the longest-ever speech, which lasted about seven minutes. Nowadays, speeches are limited to 45 seconds.

The shortest acceptance speech was by Alfred Hitchcock in 1968. All he said was: 'Thank you.'

In 1998, two British actresses were nominated for playing the same role. Dame Judi Dench played Queen Elizabeth I in *Shakespeare In Love* and Cate Blanchett played her in *Elizabeth*.

Incredibly, the film regarded by many film buffs as the best children's movie ever, *The Wizard Of Oz*, only won one Oscar in 1939.

Warren Beatty is the only person ever to be nominated for Best Producer, Director, Writer and Actor for the same film. And he's done it twice – both for 1978's *Heaven Can Wait* and for *Reds* in 1981.

Meryl Streep is the most-nominated actress, with four, although to date she has won only two Oscars.

The biggest losers among the acting profession were Richard Burton and Peter O'Toole, who both received seven Oscar nominations but never won one.

The ceremony has been postponed three times: in 1938 due to flooding in Los Angeles; in 1968 for the funeral of the Reverend Martin Luther King Jr, and in 1981 after the assassination attempt on President Ronald Reagan.

The thriller *The Silence Of The Lambs*, starring Anthony Hopkins, was the first film to be released on video before winning Best Picture in 1991.

The first posthumous Oscar winner was Sidney Howard, who won for the screenplay of *Gone With The Wind*.

The only women ever to be nominated for Best Director are Lina Wertmuller for *Seven Beauties*, Jane Campion for *The Piano* and Sophia Coppola for *Lost In Translation*.

In 1973, Marlon Brando turned down the Best Actor Oscar for his role in *The Godfather*. Instead, he sent a young woman dressed as a Native American to protest about treatment of Native Americans in movies and on television.

The biggest-ever losing films were *Turning Point* and *The Color Purple*, both of which were nominated in eleven categories but won zilch.

The only two non-professional actors to win acting Oscars are Harold Russell, for *The Best Years Of Our Lives* in 1946, and Dr Haing S. Ngor, who won in 1984 for re-living his struggle against Pol Pot in *The Killing Fields*.

The only Oscar to win an Oscar is Oscar Hammerstein II, who won Best Song in both 1941 and 1945.

The first time the Oscars were broadcast to a worldwide television audience was in 1969.

A shortage of metals in World War II meant that for three years the Oscars had to be made out of plaster. Once the war was over, the plaster figures were exchanged for gold-plated ones.

In 2000, the Oscars were stolen and found next to a bin. The dustman who found them was given tickets to the ceremony and a reward of over £25,000.

Chapter 24

SEVENTH HEAVEN

Will this year see you in seventh heaven? Or are you more likely to commit one of the Seven Deadly Sins? Will you be smooth like 007, or as dopey as one of the Seven Dwarfs? It's amazing how many times the number seven crops up in our daily lives, as the following facts reveal.

Magnificent Seven. The 1960s cult Western was a remake of *Shichinin No Samurai*, better known as *Seven Samurai*. In the Hollywood version a group of hired gunmen including screen legends Steve McQueen, Yul Brynner and Charles Bronson guard Mexican village from ruthless bandits in the 1880s.

Seven Deadly Sins: Lust, Gluttony, Greed, Sloth, Wrath, Envy and Pride. Set out by the early Christians, who warned that committing any of them condemns your soul to eternal hell.

Seven Holy Virtues: Chastity, Abstinence, Charity, Diligence, Forgiveness, Kindness and Humility. Each one is the opposite of a Deadly Sin (in the same order as above). They were taught as the golden rules for getting to heaven.

Secret Seven: Enid Blyton wrote the famous childrens' books about the adventures of a group of children who specialised in trapping crooks. They were Peter, Janet, Jack, Barbara, George, Pam, Colin, and Scamper the dog.

Seven Days of the Week: In the Bible, God created the world in six days and rested on the seventh. This seventh became the Jewish day of rest, the Sabbath. The Romans set up a seven-day week and the British Empire later spread it around the world.

Seven Wonders of the World: There have been three different lists for Ancient, Medieval and Modern Wonders. The Ancient list comprises the Great Pyramid of Giza, the Hanging Gardens of Babylon, the Temple of Artemis at Ephesus, the Statue of Zeus at Olympia, the Mausoleum of Maussollos at Halicarnassus, the Colossus of Rhodes and the Lighthouse of Alexandria. The Medieval list features Stonehenge, the Colosseum, the Catacombs of Komel Shoqafa, the Great Wall of China, the Porcelain Tower of Nanjing, the Hagia Sophia, and the Leaning Tower of Pisa. The Modern Wonders are: The Channel Tunnel, the CN Tower in Toronto, the Empire State Building, the Golden Gate Bridge, South America's Itaipu Dam, the Delta Works in the Netherlands and the Panama Canal.

Number Seven Shirt: Some of the greatest footballers ever have worn the number seven shirt, such as the superb Eric Cantona and fellow Man United legends the late, great George Best, Brian Robson and David Beckham. Liverpool and Scotland great Kenny Dalgleish wore the same number, as did Sir Stanley Matthews, the first footballer to be knighted.

Seven Continents: From biggest to smallest, Asia, Africa, North America, South America, Antarctica, Europe and Australia are Earth's seven land masses.

Lucky Number Seven: The number has long been thought to be lucky. In the Bible, it represents the union of man and woman. The biblical number for a man is four and for a woman three.

£7 billion: The personal fortune of the world's 38th richest man, Stefan Persson from Sweden. But this is small change compared with the world's richest man, Rodson Walton, the founder of the US shopping chain Walmart. His bank balance shows a whopping £45.1 billion.

007: The number of the world's most famous secret agent, James Bond. Daniel Craig is the latest super-smooth hunk, having starred as Britain's favourite spy in the Hollywood blockbuster *Casino Royale*.

Seven Seas: These vary but are usually seven out of these nine: Adriatic Sea, Aegean Sea, Arabian Sea, Black Sea, Caspian Sea, Indian Ocean, Mediterranean Sea, Persian Gulf and Red Sea. There are also seven oceans: North Pacific, South Pacific, North Atlantic, South Atlantic, Indian, Southern and Arctic.

Random Number Seven: When people are asked to pick any number between one and ten, they usually choose seven.

Seven Sides: There are seven corners on both the British 20 pence and 50 pence pieces.

Seventh Heaven: In ancient astronomy people called the Sun, Moon and the five planets visible with the naked eye the Seven Heavenly Objects. It was thought that when people died, their souls floated into the sky, visiting each of the Seven Heavenly Objects in turn until they reached the outermost layer, where they met God somewhere around Saturn.

Snow White and the Seven Dwarfs: Doc, Grumpy, Happy, Bashful, Sleepy, Dopey and Sneezy joined Snow White in the 1938 Walt Disney classic – which is still the tenth highest-grossing US film of all time nearly 70 years later.

Seven Swans a-swimming: What my true love gave to me on the seventh day of Christmas in the traditional carol. They are said to refer to the seven gifts of the Holy Spirit, the seven sacraments.

Seven Holes in the Head: There are seven openings in a human head – two ears, two nostrils, two eyes and a mouth.

Seventh Sign of the Zodiac: Libra, the Scales, is the only zodiac sign that is not a living creature.

Seven billion: The number of cigarettes smoked in the African country of Kenya in 2006.

Seven: The code for international direct dialling to Borat's homeland of Kazakhstan.

Seven million: That's the number of Londoners who live in the UK's capital city.

Seven million: The number of people in jail, on probation or on parole in America – that's 1 in every 32 US adults.

Chapter 25

HAPPY FAMILIES

There's a whole family of intriguing and inspiring facts.

MUM'S THE WORD

Mother's Day is a time for millions of marvellous mums to be spoiled with cards and masses of chocolates. No doubt about it, mums make the world go round.

The chance of a mum having twins is 1 in 33. Odds of having naturally born triplets are 1 in 7,900. For quads, it's a staggering 1 in 705,000.

August is the most popular month for having a baby, with more than 360,000 mothers giving birth that month in 2001.

Supermum Elizabeth Buttle was 19 when she had her daughter in 1956 and 60 when her next child, a son, was born in 1997. The astonishing gap of 41 years 185 days is a record for consecutive births.

Lesley Brown gave birth to the world's first test-tube baby, Louise, on 25 July 1978. Louise grew up to be a postal worker in Bristol.

The vibration of a mother cat's purring acts as a homing signal to kittens at feeding time, as they are born blind and deaf.

Movie legend Katharine Hepburn's mother was a crusader for birth control.

The mum whose baby weighed most at birth was Canadian Anna Bates, whose son tipped the scales at a whopping 23lb 12oz (10.7kg) in 1879.

Mamma mia: Maddalena Granata had fifteen sets of triplets after marrying aged 28 in Nocera, Italy, in 1867. She had 52 kids in all, only three of them girls.

Eve is credited in the Bible with being the Mother of All The Living.

Rock legend Eric Clapton was born to an unmarried mother – and to shield him from the truth he was brought up thinking his grandparents were his mum and dad and his mother was his sister.

Mother Goose is an all-time favourite character with children, featuring in story books and nursery rhymes. The first recorded mention is in a weekly French chronicle in 1660.

The mother who had the most children – an astonishing 69 – was the wife of Feodor Vassilyev in Russia. Between 1725 and 1765 she had 32 twins, seven sets of triplets and four sets of quads – and all but two of the kids survived infancy.

Only 81 per cent of women aged 40 to 44 are mums. The figure was 90 per cent in 1980.

Chinese families often honour female ancestors by having names that start with the sign for 'mother'.

A giraffe often gives birth while standing – meaning her offspring's first experience outside the womb is a 6ft (1.8m) drop.

Mother Shipton was a prophet who correctly predicted more than 400 years ago that Britain would have a Queen Elizabeth II.

Bobbi McCaughey gave birth to the first set of surviving septuplets when her four boys and three girls were delivered by Caesarean section in Iowa in 1997 after she had IVF treatment.

Madonna's mother died when the superstar singer was only five.

A mother kangaroo still has a 'reserve' embryo in her body even after her offspring settles into her pouch. It is a back-up in case the newborn joey fails to survive.

Jayne Bleackley holds the record for the shortest time between children born from separate pregnancies. Her son arrived on 3 September 1999 and daughter on 30 March 2000 – 208 days apart.

Tuesday is the most common day of the week for births.

Elvis Presley was a real mummy's boy, even sleeping in the same bed as his beloved Gladys until puberty. She walked him to and from school each day and they sometimes conversed in a baby talk only they understood.

The average age for a woman to become a mum for the first time in the UK is 24.8.

The oldest woman to give birth was 66-year-old Adriana Iliescu. She gave birth to a daughter, Eliza Maria, in Romania in 2005 after IVF.

And the world's youngest mother was Lina Medina, just five years and seven months old when she had a 6lb 8oz boy (2.9kg) in Lima, Peru, in 1939. The baby was raised as her brother and was ten before he learned Lina was his mum.

Ancient Greeks marked Mother's Day in spring, as we do today. They honoured Rhea, 'mother of the gods', with honey-cakes and drink.

British mum Mary Jonas had fifteen sets of twins – all boy-girl pairs – before she died in 1899.

A mother rabbit may abandon, ignore or even eat her young if she is frightened.

When Mothering Sunday was established, in the 1600s, servants were given time off to take a cake to their mums in a custom called 'going a-mothering'.

A mother Mexican free-tailed bat can find her young in a colony jammed with millions of babies.

Only 11 per cent of women now have four or more children – 36 per cent did in 1976.

Anna Jarvis campaigned for Mother's Day to be a US holiday in 1914 – then moaned it was too commercialised.

FATHER, DEAR FATHER

On Father's Day, shops sell out of terrible ties, car-cleaning kits and rotten aftershave. And even if you manage to find the perfect card for your old man, what do you write in it? How can you sum up in a few words what your Dad means to you? And what's going through your Pa's mind? Here's what some famous names have had to say about their dads.

'I never want to have children. I just wouldn't want another me.' – Simon Cowell

'Kids cost a lot, don't they? Maybe we can get one who's 22 and a solicitor so he can bring a good wage in.' – Ricky Gervais

'I won't lie to you. Fatherhood is not easy like motherhood.' – Homer Simpson

'When I was a kid, I said to my father one afternoon: "Daddy, will you take me to the zoo?" He answered: "If the zoo wants you, let them come and get you."' – Jerry Lewis

'Father's Day always worries me. I'm afraid I'll get something I can't afford.' – Billy Connolly

'I am often asked whether it's because of some genetic trait that I stand with my hands behind me, like my father. The answer is that we both have the same tailor. He makes our sleeves so tight we can't get our hands in front.' – Prince Charles

'Why does a man want a child? Is it to perpetuate the species? Is the child a pet substitute? Is it to prove he has had sex at least once?' – Jeremy Hardy

'My father had a profound influence on me. He was a lunatic.' – Spike Milligan

'I love fatherhood. I love the girls and they take precedence over everything because, from the minute they're born, they love you and they're helpless without you. I want to be a good dad and I worry about it all the time.' – James Nesbitt

'My father was an amazing man. The older I got, the smarter he got.' – Mark Twain

'Every single day of my life is significantly better because I'm a father. I cannot understand how I managed to cope without getting cuddled this many times a day.' – Russell Crowe

'I'm a decrepit father made lame by fortune's spite.' – William Shakespeare

'Fatherhood is great but there is one problem. She doesn't sleep. At night she seems to turn into a vampire. She wakes up every night five or ten times, asking for things, singing, calling out.' – Tennis ace Goran Ivanisevic on his daughter

'Warren Beatty only had children so he could meet some babysitters.' – David Letterman

'As a child, I thought I hated everybody, but when I grew up I realised it was just children I didn't like.' – Poet Philip Larkin

'You look into the eyes of children the whole time and think what their prospects are going to be.' – Gordon Brown

'It's a wonderful feeling when your father becomes not a god but a man to you – when he comes down from the mountain and you see he's this man with weaknesses. And you love him as a human being, not just as a figurehead.' – Robin Williams

'You have to be mad to have children. The less you know about what it will really be like, the better, otherwise no one would ever do it.' – Nigel Planer

'Typical of Margaret. She produced twins and avoided the necessity of a second pregnancy.' – Denis Thatcher

'I just stared at myself in the mirror and kept saying: "What the f*** now? You're going to be a father." But then I wondered would I do all right? I knew it was the long haul, and I thought: "Why not? It's going to be a hoot!"' – Sir Bob Geldof

'A father is the guy who's quick to appear with the camera and just as quick to disappear when there's a nappy to be changed.' – Joan Rivers

'I really want to have a child because Christmas without one is rubbish.' – Hugh Grant

'Money – the one thing that keeps us in touch with our children.' – Gyles Brandreth

'Fatherhood was an invigorating, frightening upheaval. It is the most unpredictably wild thing that ever happened to me.' – Colin Firth

'Have you any idea how difficult it is to be a father? Children forget that although they have no previous experience of being children, their fathers have no previous experience of being fathers.' – Peter Ustinov

Ernie: 'Are you of royal stock?'
Eric: 'No, my father was a grocer. I'm of vegetable stock.'
– Morecambe and Wise

'I was born in very sorry circumstances. My mother was sorry and my father was sorry as well.'
– Norman Wisdom

'I felt something impossible for me to explain in words when my daughter was born. Then, when they took her away, it hit me. I got scared all over again and began to feel giddy. Then it came to me… I was a father.' – Nat King Cole

'My dad used to say: "It's not a sin to be skint, but it's a sin to look skint."' – Alan Ball

'When the kids have their friends round, I have to pretend to be Fun Dad so they won't go back to their parents and say: "He was really shouty."' – Jonathan Ross

'I can do one of two things: I can be President of the United States or I can control my daughter. I cannot possibly do both.' – Theodore Roosevelt

'Being a dad is more important than football.' – David Beckham

'I don't like children, but I like to make them.' – Groucho Marx

'Being a father is the hardest job in the world. You try to lead your kids up the right path, but who am I to lead anybody up the f***ing path? How can I give out the rules when I'm worse than them most of the time? When you see me coming home in police cars, in f****ing ambulances, in straitjackets and chains?' – Ozzy Osbourne

Chapter 26

IT'S ABOUT TIME

'Just a second...' 'Hang on a minute.' We all uses phrases like these every day without really thinking about them. A second seems like nothing – a tiny, meaningless moment in time. But you'd be amazed at just how much can happen in a single second, or two, or three. And you'd be even more amazed at how much goes on in one hour in the life of Britain.

EVERY SECOND

£1,117 is spent in Tesco – that's more than £2,937,422,931 per month.

Two new Internet blogs or web diaries are created. Most British bloggers post between 6pm and 10pm.

EVERY TWO SECONDS

94 Kit Kats are bought – that's nearly 1.5 billion a year.

EVERY THREE SECONDS

We eat eighteen chicken sandwiches.

EVERY FOUR SECONDS

925 bananas are eaten – nearly 140 million a week.

EVERY FIVE SECONDS

1,410 credit or debit card transactions take place.

EVERY SIX SECONDS

A jar of Nivea, Joan Collins's favourite face cream, is bought.

EVERY SEVEN SECONDS

An item of women's clothing sells on eBay in the UK.

EVERY EIGHT SECONDS

Seven people trespass on railway property.

EVERY NINE SECONDS

We eat 8,500 potatoes.

EVERY TEN SECONDS

Someone buys Premium Bonds.

There is an accident on British roads.

EVERY ELEVEN SECONDS

3,350 avocados are sold in the UK.

EVERY TWELVE SECONDS

Bookie William Hill loses fifteen of those little pens used to fill out betting slips.

EVERY THIRTEEN SECONDS

A garment of menswear sells on eBay in the UK.

EVERY FOURTEEN SECONDS

More than £375 is stolen on the Internet and by phone and fax.

EVERY FIFTEEN SECONDS

Two people commit adultery.

EVERY SIXTEEN SECONDS

We swallow over 1,000 Smarties.

EVERY SEVENTEEN SECONDS

We eat 330,000 eggs.

EVERY EIGHTEEN SECONDS

We drink 64 gallons (290 litres) of alcohol.

EVERY NINETEEN SECONDS

Nine nervous learner drivers start their test. Just four will pass.

EVERY TWENTY SECONDS

A cleavage-enhancing Wonderbra is sold.

EVERY 30 SECONDS

We chomp 8,333 packets of crisps.

EVERY MINUTE

An immigrant arrives in the UK.

Police receive a 999 call about domestic violence.

We send an estimated 100,000 text messages.

EVERY TWO MINUTES

One person in the UK suffers a heart attack – that works out to 720 every day.

Someone is mugged.

EVERY THREE MINUTES

Two planes take off from Heathrow Airport.

Someone goes bankrupt.

A married couple is divorced.

EVERY FOUR MINUTES

The UK population's collective personal debt goes up by £1 million.

Someone dies from a smoking-related disease.

EVERY FIVE MINUTES

A UK citizen emigrates.

EVERY SIX MINUTES

A driver is caught speeding.

EVERY SEVEN MINUTES

A teacher is verbally or physically abused by a pupil.

EVERY EIGHT MINUTES

A pensioner dies during the winter months.

EVERY NINE MINUTES

750 bottles of champagne are drunk in the UK.

EVERY TEN MINUTES

A child will be admitted to hospital suffering from asthma, the biggest children's disease in the UK.

More than 10,400 creatures – mice, hamsters and other furry animals – are killed by pet cats.

EVERY FIFTEEN MINUTES

More than 1,000 rats are born in London.

EVERY TWENTY MINUTES

We use 112,000 disposable nappies – just over 8 million every day.

More than 15 people are reported missing to the National Missing Persons Helpline. The vast majority return within 72 hours.

EVERY 30 MINUTES

More than 5,000 vehicles pass through Britain's busiest A-road and junction – the Hangar Lane gyratory in London, where the A406 North Circular meets the A40.

A book is abandoned on the London Underground.

Speed cameras catch almost 30,000 speeding drivers.

EVERY 45 MINUTES

We eat just over 98.2 tons (99,775kg) of chips.

More than eight hedgehogs are killed on British roads.

EVERY HOUR

At least one stray dog is put down.

An estimated 240 vehicle break-ins are attempted.

Just over 41 smokers quit for good.

A London house goes up in value by £3.76 – an increase of around £33,000 per year.

A man is killed by prostate cancer.

An under-18 is admitted to hospital for alcohol abuse.

More than 14,500 passengers pass through Heathrow Airport.

The UK produces 47,945 tons (48,714,369kg) of solid waste – enough to fill the Albert Hall.

A rape or sexual assault takes place in London.

We eat nearly 110 tonnes (110,000kg) of chocolate.

74 babies are born.

We eat about 20 tonnes (20,000kg) of sausages, worth £55,559.

UK homes receive more than 270,000 silent calls.

Nearly £9,000 is spent on gambling – triple the figure of five years ago.

Running a car costs the average motorist £1.20.

More than 208,333 customers are served in the UK's 1,200 branches of McDonald's.

We spend £2,495,218 on builders, cleaners and gardeners.

Just over 23 books are published.

Chapter 27

KIDS' TALK

One day I told my small son Harry that next day, Friday, was pay day, to which he replied: 'Dad, if you only get paid on Fridays, why do you work all those other days?'

'Mummy,' said Bethany just before I was due to give birth to her brother, 'you're getting really fat.'
'I know darling,' I replied patting my stomach. 'That's because I have a baby in my tummy.'
She had a good look at my behind. 'Well, what have got in your bottom, then?'

My great-niece wanted to know how old I was.
'I don't know,' I said mischievously.

'You ought to know how old you are,' she said. 'I know how old I am.'
'Well,' I said, 'I must have forgotten.'
'Look in your knickers, granny,' she said.
'In my knickers?' I repeated, puzzled. 'How will that help?'
'It tells you how old you are on the label. Mine says "For a five- to seven-year-old".'

'One day, Mummy,' said Lauren, 'I want to get married.'
'Well, he'll be a very lucky boy,' I replied.
'I'm not getting married yet,' she said horrified. 'You have to be really old and if you pick the wrong person you're stuck with him for the rest of your life.'
'You mean like me and Daddy?' I asked jokingly.
'Exactly,' she replied.

My daughter Rachel, a bridesmaid at her sister Sally's wedding, was all ears when the vicar asked the bride: 'Do you take this man for better or worse, for richer or poorer, in sickness and in health?'
'Say richer,' she whispered.

My grandson and I were playing with his Lego on the carpet and as I bent down over the pieces I was building, he said: 'Grandad, did you know that the top of your head is growing through your hair?'

My daughter Hayley used to spend a long time playing in the bath when she was young. One day, when she eventually got out, her toes were red and wrinkled. She stared at them and said: 'I'm all shrinkled!'

My husband John once asked my son Trevor: 'Have I ever lied to you?'
'Well,' he replied. 'You did about Father Christmas.'

I was playing tennis with my seven-year-old daughter when she stopped me in my tracks by saying: 'You know, Mum, if it wasn't for your face, you'd look about nineteen.'

When he was ten, I brought my son Michael over to the UK on holiday. One day we had bought our tickets and were running for a train. A porter said: 'Rushing, are you?'
Michael, with an amazed look on his face, said: 'No, we're from Canada.'

On the way to Brownies, my daughter Lucy, aged seven, told her dad before he picked up her two pals:

'Daddy before we set off, can we get something straight – no singing in front of my friends.'

When a friend of mine died I sent a card and after her name I wrote RIP. 'What does RIP mean, Granny?' asked my grandson Michael.
'Each letter stands for a word,' I told him.
'Return If Possible?' he asked.

My godson Chris was in Sunday school when the vicar, thinking of grace, asked the class: 'Does anyone know what is said before you eat?'
'I know what my dad says,' answered Harry. 'Go easy on the butter.'

As I was reading the story of Peter Pan to my granddaughter Emma, aged four, she asked: 'Grandad, what did they call Captain Hook before he lost his arm?'

'You might not be as tall as Daddy,' said my young son Nathan to his Uncle Michael, 'but you're a lot, lot wider.'

My next-door neighbour's eight-year-old girl Juliet came home after visiting her new baby brother in hospital. She told me: 'He won't be home just yet because he's very small and has to be kept in an incinerator.'

After looking at some old black-and-white photographs, my son John sat next to his grandma and asked: 'Were you alive when the world was black and white?'

In the doctor's surgery, my grandson David approached an elderly man in a wheelchair and asked him: 'Can you do wheelies in that?'

My son, a little Yorkshire tyke aged ten, lost a tooth and that night put it under his pillow.
'I'm surprised that you still believe in the Tooth Fairy,' I said.
'I'll believe owt,' he replied, 'if there's money in it.'

A teacher read the story of Little Red Riding Hood and then asked the children to write the story in their own words. My six-year-old daughter wrote: 'Little Red Riding Hood had bright red tits.' When the teacher questioned her later, he discovered that she meant 'tights'.

My young nephew had been learning about evolution and asked: 'Nanna, did you used to be a monkey?'

Chapter 28

TRUTH OR FICTION?

Some stories are so off the wall that you just know they must be a load of old junk – or are they? In fact a lot of old wives' tales that sound complete nonsense are really completely true. And even many tales that have been handed down over the years actually have a basis in fact.

A giraffe has exactly the same number of bones in its neck as a human. Strangely, the number is seven even though a giraffe's neck is 5–6ft (1.5–1.8m) long and ours only a few inches (but a giraffe's neck bones are each 10in – 25cm – long). In fact, all mammals have seven neck vertebrae and scientists say this proves we all came from one shared ancestor.

Hollywood screen hunk Clark Gable was registered as a girl at birth by mistake after the registrar misread the doctor's scrawled writing.

Men have a higher pain threshold than women. Tests have shown that because women's skin is thinner, the difference in blood flow ensures they feel more pain.

King Richard II married Isabella of Valois, daughter of the French King Charles VI, when she was just seven years old in 1396. He was a widower of 27 at the time, having married his first wife Anne of Bohemia when he was fifteen.

Coca-Cola used to contain cocaine. The recipe has always been secret, but the drink was first made in the nineteenth century using the coca leaf, from which the drug is made. The modern-day fizzy drink has now dropped this ingredient.

Queen Victoria's hubby Prince Albert had a genital piercing – known these days as a... Prince Albert. Although many assume the nickname for penis rings came long after his death, they were quite common in the Victorian court. Male courtiers wore tight-fitting legwear. As with modern-day cycle shorts, it would have been noticeable if they were out of place. So a genital ring was used to attach male members to the inside legs, out of the way.

Earwigs are so called because they crawl into people's ears. When we used to sleep on pillows stuffed with straw, earwigs would crawl out and mistake ears holes for their natural hiding places of small, round, dark crevices. But there is no truth in the story that they used to go on to bore into people's brains to lay their eggs.

Chocolate is poisonous to dogs and as little as 3oz (85g) could be fatal to a 25lb (11.3kg) dog. The reason is that it passes through the dog's body very slowly, taking about seventeen hours to get rid of chemicals that attack its nervous system. Humans get rid of it in less than six hours. Don't worry about special dog treat chocolate that are sold in pet shops, though. They are only chocolate flavoured.

Oysters used to be a poor man's food, not reserved for the rich and served on silver salvers. Now considered a delicacy, in Victorian London they cost around two-and-six for 100 and were tossed in cooking pots by the bucketload and boiled up as a teatime snack. Overfishing later made them a rarity.

In nineteenth-century England, men sold their wives. Although it was illegal and punishable by a month in jail with hard labour, there are several records of such sales. In 1852, Carlisle farmer Joseph Thomson asked 50 shillings for his 'spruce and lively damsel' Mary Anne, 22 – but only got 20. And in the 1820s a Brighton man accepted 30 shillings for his 'tidy-looking woman', who arrived at the auction wearing a halter round her neck.

It might put you off your tea, but bone China is really made from bones. What makes it different from other types of ceramic is the addition of real animal-bone ash.

'Red sky at night, shepherd's delight. Red sky at morning, shepherd's warning' is one of the best ways to forecast weather. The sun sets in the west and that's where our weather comes from. So if the sky is clear and we can see the sunset, tomorrow is likely to be fine. But the sun rises in the east, so if the sky is clear there, the good weather has probably passed and worse will follow.

Male seahorses have babies: While the female produces the eggs, she then pops them into a pouch on the underside of the male's tail. But this is not just a babysitting role. The male actually feeds the young through a placenta inside the pouch and they stay there until they hatch. And just to prove that men make less fuss, the male will usually become 'pregnant' again within 48 hours of giving birth.

An apple a day could kill you. Far from keeping the doctor at bay, if you eat the whole fruit mushed up into a smoothy, you risk illness or even death. Why? The pips contain the deadly poison cyanide.

Concentration camps were a British, not German, invention. Though they are associated with Nazi atrocities in World War II, they were first used by Brits during the Boer War in South Africa. In 1902, 60,000 prisoners were kept in them.

Scientific genius Albert Einstein was a flop as a schoolboy. Although he's now considered one of the greatest brains of the last century he was expelled from his first school and failed most of his exams at his second.

Bulgarians shake their heads to mean yes and nod their heads to mean no. Some Bulgarians, however, realise that this is confusing foreigners, so they nod for yes and shake for no as we do. All you have to do is work out which sort of Bulgarian you are looking at.

Bananas are radioactive. So are Brazil nuts and mussels. The everyday foods contain high levels of radium. Don't worry, though. One Brazil nut, for example, contains 0.1 microsieverts compared to a chest X-ray's 8,000.

Don't try this at home – but a crocodile's jaws can be held shut by a human hand. Oddly, the muscles that open the jaws are very weak. But once open they can snap shut with a force of 3,000lb (1,360kg) per square inch.

TAKING THE MYTH

They're the nagging questions you're never sure about and it's anyone's guess whether they're right or wrong. Well now we can help. Thanks to some fascinating websites it's now possible to tell fact from fiction at the click of a mouse.

Marilyn Monroe had six toes on her left foot.
False: Photos published in 1991 seemed to show the Hollywood star with six toes on her left foot. But there are lots of other pictures that show the normal five.

You can't fold a piece of paper in half more than seven times.
False: In 2002, US student Britney Gallivan folded a 4,000ft-long (1,219m) toilet roll in half an amazing twelve times.

A mouse can fit through a hole as wide as a pencil.
True: House mice have a soft skull and a slim, flexible body, which means that they can squeeze themselves through the tiniest of gaps.

Eating a stick of celery burns more calories than it contains.
True: An average celery stick has about six calories, but as they are in the form of cellulose, humans can't digest them so they have zero nutritional value. But eating the celery does burn a tiny number of calories, so there is a net loss.

Your hair can turn grey overnight.
False: Hair turns white with age due to fall in pigment production, but it is a slow process and does not happen overnight. Experts think early greying may be due to a deficiency in vitamins or copper.

Men have a higher sex drive than women.
False: Nature may have made men more promiscuous by giving them twenty times more testosterone than women. But a recent survey among women travelling on the London Tube found that 42 per cent thought about sex on their way to work, while only 22 per cent of men did.

As we get older we shrink.
True: Osteopaths say our skeletal frame reaches peak density at about 30, then it's a long, slow process of shrinkage. You can expect to lose about an inch (2.5cm) of your height by the time you are 70.

It is illegal to burn money.
False: Defacing banknotes or coins is an offence under the Currency and Bank Notes Act 1928 – because you could still try to spend them after they are changed. But once a banknote is burnt it is gone forever, has no value and only you are the loser.

A bowl of pub peanuts contains traces of 100 different types of urine.
False: It's just a yucky urban myth. But a 2003 study by the UK Health Protection Agency did find that 44 per cent of ice that came from pubs and restaurants contained coliform bacteria, which is passed out in human faeces. Ugh.

TV chef Delia Smith baked the cake on the sleeve of the Rolling Stones' *Let It Bleed* album.
True: Delia was working as a home economist in 1969 when she was commissioned to bake a cake for a photo shoot. She later said she had been told to make it 'very over-the-top and as gaudy as I could'.

You can be electrocuted by talking on a mobile phone in a thunderstorm.
True: TV presenters Jamie Hyneman and Adam Savage proved this is true this using a dummy and 200,000 volts of electricity.

Author Salman Rushdie wrote the 'Naughty But Nice' slogan for cream cake ads.
True: The *Satanic Verses* writer worked for an ad agency in the 1970s. He also came up with 'Irresistabubble' for Aero choc bars.

In Switzerland, it's illegal to flush the loo after 10pm.
False: Some blocks of flats do have tough anti-noise pollution rules such as these, but nowhere is it set down as a law.

Daddy longlegs can deliver a deadly bite
False: This was tested by letting hundreds of Daddy longlegs swarm all over peoples' bodies. One bite was recorded, which left a tiny lump, but it disappeared almost straight away.

Tarantulas shatter if dropped.
True: The hairy spiders may look soft and furry, but they have amazingly fragile bodies. Even a fall from a few centimetres will break most of its exoskeleton or burst its belly.

A mobile phone could cause an explosion at a petrol station.
False: A mobile phone couldn't possibly set off an electrostatic discharge (i.e. a spark) to ignite petrol fumes.

Silicone breasts explode at high altitudes or low pressure.
False: Boob implants adapt to many different

environments and will not explode when you jet off on holiday.

A Polar Bear's fur is colourless.
True: It is actually transparent, so it reflects light around it – white in the day and orange at sunset.

A penny dropped off the top of a skyscraper would slice through anyone below.
False: It would not even penetrate the skin if it were fired from a rifle.

Covering a naked body with gold paint (the fate of Shirley Eaton's character in Bond film *Goldfinger*) will cause death by asphyxiation.
False: The worst anyone undergoing this experiment are flu-like symptoms.

Chapter 29

DUMB AND DUMBER

Our newspapers are filled every day with tales of the eccentricities of life in Britain so outlandish you wouldn't believe them unless they were written down in black and white. The following strange but true tales will raise a laugh even when the headlines are doom-laden.

Wight wallies

Isle of Wight Council splashed out £600 to buy thinking caps for its bosses – so they could dream up money-saving ideas. Another £1,200 was used to buy 3,000 puzzles that formed cubes spelling the word 'Think'. An insider said: 'There's not one brain cell between them.'

Guy Dorks

Guy Fawkes was banned by politically correct council chiefs at Tower Hamlets, London – and replaced with a Bengali folk tale at a cost of £75,000.

As-d'oh!

Plymouth City Council asked a family to keep a diary on antisocial neighbours then sent it to the troublemakers by mistake – forcing the entire family to move for their own protection.

Park and hide

Grandad Ken Stevenson had waited a YEAR for a disabled parking space outside his house. But 24 hours after he finally got it, Portland Council in Dorset laid tarmac on top of it, wiping it out. 'It's the most stupid thing I've ever heard,' said a pal.

S-light work

A worker who fixed broken street light bulbs in Birmingham was off sick for a year, but his bosses at Birmingham City Council still paid him more than £91,000. Lucky Ian Smith received a basic salary of £71,000, plus a bonus of £15,668 – and even £5,000 in overtime.

Shetland phonies

Shetland councillors clocked-up £100,000 of expenses – not to mention lots of CO_2 emissions – on going to environmental conferences in the Caribbean, Madeira, Crete, Paris, Madrid and New York. 'It's a disgrace,' environmentalists fumed.

Blooming madness

Most gardens in a run-down estate were full of rubbish, broken electrical goods and even old cars. One garden was well kept. So Castle Morpeth Borough Council in Northumberland sent a letter warning its owner that his garden was spoiling the area.

Killer doormats

All homeowners were told to get rid of their doormats by Bristol City Council – because, they said, there was a risk of tripping over them.

Junked mail

Careful Andy Tierney thought he was doing the right thing by disposing of some junk mail in a litter bin, doing his bit to keep the streets tidy. Hinckley and Bosworth Borough Council didn't. They slapped him with a £50 fine, claiming that he was breaching the Environmental Protection Act.

Banana twits

A driver dropped a banana skin out of his car window – and Braintree District Council lost £1,000 of taxpayer's cash in court costs by unsuccessfully trying to prosecute him.

Nab a granny

When an 80-year-old gran paid her council flat rent, she made a mistake and was short by just five pence. So Greater Manchester Council sent a burly bailiff round to her home to demand the 'arrears'.

Faraway fee

A weekend training course for thirteen councillors cost Basildon Council in Essex £3,000, including hotel rooms just 8 miles (12.8km) from its offices.

Taking the mike

As a children's motorbike display team performed at a carnival in West End, near Southampton, Tory councillor Steve Broomfield from Eastleigh Borough Council moaned: 'Oh no, they're not doing this again. Get them off – they're crap. This is so boring.' Unfortunately for him, he had left the microphone switched on and his comments were broadcast for all to hear over the PA system.

Safe as houses

A convicted murderer was given a job as a housing officer – with access to council tenants' homes – by North Warwickshire Borough Council, who failed to make full checks on his background.

Going conkers

Kids chucking sticks and stones up trees to collect conkers was considered dangerous by Worcester Council, so they paid workmen £100 a tree to strip them bare and avoid insurance claims. They left the conkers on the ground, though, so kids could still play with them.

Must try harder

Workmen from Leeds City Council did a lovely job repainting warning signs on the road outside a school. The only problem was, it had been demolished in 2003. Taxpayers in Otley, West Yorkshire, complained bitterly: 'It's a mind-blowing waste of our money.'

Deadly damages

A road accident victim was killed in a collision with a lamppost, but officials at Middlesbrough Council sent him a bill for damaging the post. They later realised their mistake and cancelled the debt.

Meating of minds

Kids at four Church of England schools were served halal meat for seventeen years without their parents' knowing – thanks to 'politically correct' Reading Borough Council.

Pushing the vote out

Eleven BNP councillors at Barking and Dagenham didn't back a measure they had proposed themselves – because they missed the vote.

Land scrape

When their street was landscaped after an eight-year battle in Washingborough, Lincolnshire, residents cheered. They stopped just three hours later, however, when council contractors arrived and dug the whole lot up again.

I've bin picked on

Mum-of-three Donna Chalice was dragged into court by Exeter City Council for putting the wrong rubbish in her recycling bin. Donna, 30, said: 'I can't be the only one.'

Hair-brained

Binge drinking in city centres was a problem for Bath

and North East Somerset council, so they launched a fierce crackdown – by ordering hairdressers to stop serving wine to women waiting for their perms.

Brew couldn't make it up

To save money, East Herts Council fired its tea lady – then hired a £200-a-day consultant to teach staff how to make a cuppa for themselves. One employee said: 'The council needs to let off some steam.'

Chapter 30

CELEBRITY WISDOM

To show that stars aren't all overpaid and underbrained, here's a selection of wise words from the great and the good.

MONEY

'Money doesn't make you happy. I now have $50million but I was just as happy when I had $48million.' – Arnold Schwarzenegger

'Money talks but all mine ever says is goodbye.' – Anonymous

'A fool and his money are lucky to have met in the first place.' – W.C. Fields

'Money is like manure, you have to spread it around or it smells.' – John Paul Getty

ANIMALS

'Dogs look up to you, cats look down on you. Pigs treat you as equal.' – Winston Churchill

'Fish like cheese… some fish.' – Ozzy Osbourne

'Yesterday I was a dog. Today I'm a dog. Tomorrow I'll probably still be a dog. (Sigh) There's so little hope for advancement.' – Snoopy

'All animals are equal but some animals are more equal than others.' – George Orwell

SEX

'Orgasms don't last long enough.' – Courtney Cox

'Love is the answer – but while you're waiting for the answer, sex raises some pretty good questions.' – Woody Allen

'Sex is 50 per cent what you've got and 50 per cent what people think you've got.' – Sophia Loren

'You know why blondes have more fun? They are easier to find in the dark.' – Dolly Parton

SUCCESS

'Success is a great deodorant.' – Elizabeth Taylor

'If you really want something in this life, you have to work hard for it. Now quiet, they're about to announce the lottery numbers.' – Homer Simpson

'You have to be a bastard to make it and that's a fact.' – John Lennon

'The only place where success comes before work is in the dictionary.' – Vidal Sassoon

'I don't know the key to success but the key to failure is to try to please everyone.' – Bill Cosby

'It's true that hard work never killed anyone but, I figure, why take the chance?' – Ronald Reagan

'Show me a good loser and I'll show you a loser.' – Paul Newman

'A man who, after the age of 30, finds himself on a bus can count himself a failure in life.' – Margaret Thatcher

MARRIAGE

'Always get married early in the morning. That way, if it doesn't work out, you haven't wasted a whole day.' – Mickey Rooney

'Marriage is too interesting an experiment to be tried only once.' – Eva Gabor

'Marriage is an institution but who wants to live in an institution?' – Groucho Marx

'There's only one way to have a happy marriage and as soon as I learn what it is, I'll marry again.' – Clint Eastwood

'If you want to sacrifice the admiration of many men for the criticism of one, go ahead, get married.' – Katharine Hepburn

'I know nothing about sex because I was always married.' – Zsa Zsa Gabor

DRINK

'An alcoholic is someone you don't like who drinks as much as you do.' – Dylan Thomas

'I only drink to steady my nerves. And sometimes I get so steady that I don't move for several months.' – W.C. Fields

'I hate to advocate drugs, alcohol, violence or insanity to anyone, but they've always worked for me.' – Hunter S. Thompson

'If you drink, don't drive. Don't even putt.' – Dean Martin

'What I don't like about office Christmas parties is looking for a job the next day.' – Phyllis Diller

'The problem with people who have no vices is that generally they have some pretty annoying virtues.' – Elizabeth Taylor

FAMILY

'Never have children, only grandchildren.' – Gore Vidal

'Be nice to your children, for they will choose your rest home.' – Phyllis Diller

'Get your brother in the band. Punch his head every now and then.' – Noel Gallagher on Liam

'Parents were invented to make children happy by giving them something to ignore.' – Ogden Nash

FRIENDS

'A friend in need is a pest. Get rid of him.' – Tommy Cooper

'Friendship is the hardest thing in the world to explain. It's not something you learn in school. But if you haven't learned the meaning of friendship, you really haven't learned anything.' – Muhammad Ali

'My mother used to say that there are no strangers, only friends you haven't met yet. She's now in a maximum-security twilight home in Australia.' – Dame Edna Everage

'Money can't buy you friends, but you get a better class of enemies.' – Spike Milligan

'True friends stab you in the front.' – Oscar Wilde

LIFE

'If you are going through hell, keep going.' – Sir Winston Churchill

'That which does not kill us makes us stronger.' – Friedrich Nietzsche

'Start every day with a smile and get it over with.' – W.C. Fields

'There's no cure for life.' – Johnny Cash

'The tragedy of life is what dies in a man while he lives.' – Albert Einstein

'Smile. Tomorrow will be worse.' – Woody Allen

CELEBRITY BACK-STABBERS

Prior to a recent Oscars ceremony, US chat show host David Letterman joked: 'We can expect a lot of new faces at the Academy Awards. Not a lot of new people, but a lot of new faces.' Do we feel sorry for the rich and famous on the receiving end of Letterman's attack? Do we heck. The stars have always been good at sniping – and they're more than capable of giving and taking it. Here are some of the best put-downs, insults and tongue-lashings the stars have handed out to each other.

'Actor Arnold Schwarzenegger looks like a condom full of walnuts.' – TV presenter Clive James

'ABI Titmuss? She's been tied to more bedposts than David Blunkett's dog.' – Jonathan Ross

'Really no surprise that Bob Geldof's such an expert on famine. He has, after all, been dining out on "I Don't Like Mondays" for 30 years.' – Russell Brand

'A lot of people use two-piece snooker cues. Alex Higgins doesn't, though, because they don't come with instructions.' – Steve Davis

'I've met serial killers and assassins but nobody scared me as much as Mrs Thatcher.' – Ken Livingstone

'Joe Frazier is so ugly he should donate his face to the US Bureau of Wildlife.' – Muhammad Ali

'Julia Roberts has a very big mouth. When I kissed her I was aware of a slight echo.' – Hugh Grant on his *Notting Hill* co-star

'I don't dislike Robbie Williams. I don't hate him. I just think he's rubbish.' – Liam Gallagher

'Robbie Williams? You mean that fat dancer from Take That?' – Noel Gallagher

'Congratulations, Madge, on your lovely little black baby David. Are you stopping there, or getting more? When I went to Africa, all I got was a wallet.' – Jonathan Ross

'Sir Elton John's writing is limited to songs for dead blondes.' – Keith Richards

'Boy George is all England needs – another queen who can't dress.' – Joan Rivers

'Joan Collins looks like she combs her hair with an eggbeater.' – Louella Parsons

'Is Billy Idol just doing a bad Elvis pout, or was he born that way?' – Freddie Mercury

'Unlike Cheryl Cole and the girls, I have co-written seven of my album tracks. I fail to see how that means I have copied their sound. I mean, I haven't resorted to wearing short skirts and dating a footballer to get into the charts, now have I?' – Charlotte Church on Girls Aloud

'Charlotte Church is a nasty little piece of work with a fat head. Her publicity stunts slagging everyone off haven't worked. I don't know who she and her scabby boyfriend think they are. He's a posing idiot who looks like a girl. And she's not even gorgeous.' – Cheryl Cole replies to Charlotte

'You're a liar and a fake. You're not in Neverland here. You're not no princess here. You're normal. You are normal Shilpa and learn to live with it.' – Jade Goody to Shilpa Shetty on *Celebrity Big Brother*

'Michael Jackson's album was called *Bad* because there wasn't enough room on the sleeve for Pathetic.' – Prince

'Madonna is so hairy, when she lifted up her arm, I thought it was Tina Turner in her armpit.' – Joan Rivers

'I'm glad Abi Titmuss did *Love Island* because finally the world has seen how pig ugly she is… She's got four chins and a beer gut and it's all airbrushed out of the pictures in the lads' mags.' – Jodie Marsh

'Princess Anne is such an active lass. So out-doorsy. She loves nature in spite of what it did to her.' – Bette Midler

'John McEnroe was as charming as always, which means that he was as charming as a dead mouse in a loaf of bread.' – Clive James

'Shane Richie? He's just a f**king holiday redcoat.' – *EastEnder* Steve McFadden

'Chevy Chase couldn't ad-lib a fart after a baked-bean dinner.' – Johnny Carson

'The Russians love Brooke Shields. It's because her eyebrows remind them of Leonid Brezhnev.' – Robin Williams

'Caprice is cold, calculating, inanimate… I call her the cash register.' – John McCrick on his fellow *Celebrity Big Brother* contestant

'If I found Yoko Ono floating in my pool, I'd punish my dog.' – Joan Rivers

'The easiest way for you to lose 10lb is just to take off your wig.' – Madonna to Elton John

'Who let the dogs out?' – Victoria Beckham on seeing Jordan

'Most of the time Marlon Brando sounds like he has a mouth full of toilet paper.' – Rex Reed

'You can calculate Zsa Zsa Gabor's age by the rings on her fingers.' – Bob Hope

'Trevor Brooking floats like a butterfly… and stings like one too.' – Brian Clough

'Prince looks like he's been dipped in a bucket of pubic hair.' – Boy George

Chapter 31

DOCTOR, DOCTOR!

Most of us just ask our GP for something to cure a bad cough or a sore toe, but there are so many more interesting things you could quiz your doc about. Like why your fingers go wrinkly in the bath. Or why onions make you cry. For the answers to some of life's trickier questions, read on.

Do your ears keep growing after the rest of you stops?

Yes, but that's the least of your worries: As we get older, all this happens to our faces: Muscle tone is lost, causing that saggy look and double chin; your nose grows longer, your skin wrinkles, and your hair goes grey; you get droopy eyes, receding gums, missing teeth… and bigger ears. They do keep growing but only a bit, probably due to cartilage growth.

Can you lose a contact lens in the back of your head?

Panicking lens wearers regularly turn up in casualty departments convinced that their lens has slipped behind their eyes into the back of their heads. In fact they are often found folded and tucked up under the eyelid. But if they can't be found, where are they? Probably on the bathroom floor at home, because there is nowhere else for lenses to go.

What are hiccups and how do you get rid of them?

Hiccups are when your diaphragm – the muscle that separates your lungs from your stomach – becomes irritated and pushes air rapidly upwards. Too much food, alcohol or air can bring on an attack, as can excitement or stress. Touted cures include breathing into a paper bag, holding your breath, drinking water through a straw with your fingers in your ears, or placing a cotton bud in your mouth and gently rubbing and pulling your tongue hard.

Does masturbation cause stuttering, blindness or hairy palms?

Whatever you read or are told when caught as a youngster is not true at all. In fact, a recent study showed that men who masturbate more than 21 times a month had a lower risk of prostate cancer.

Why do you cry when you peel onions?

Simple: Cutting an onion releases an enzyme called lachrymatory-factor synthase. This reacts with the onion to produce sulfenic acids, which immediately turn into synpropanethial-S-oxide. When this hits your eyes it triggers nerve fibres that activate tear glands. Heating onions, peeling under the tap, or wearing goggles are meant to help... or you could just order a take-away.

Why *do* men have nipples?

All babies are girls for about the first six weeks in the womb and only after that does the male sex chromosome kick in for boys. The embryo then begins to develop all its male characteristics, but men are left with nipples and some breast tissue from those early days. Men can even get breast cancer and there are even some medical conditions that can cause male breasts to enlarge into 'man boobs'.

Why do fingers go wrinkly in the bath?

When we have a good old soak, the outer layer of our skin (the epidermis) absorbs a little water and expands. But the layer of skin below this does not swell, so the skin buckles. Skin on the hands and feet is thicker than on the rest of the body, and so the wrinkles are more noticeable.

Is it dangerous to hold it when you have to pee?

A full bladder ruptures more easily than an empty one, but this doesn't mean yours will explode if you hold it. Our bodies have an automatic mechanism called the micturition reflex to stop our bladder getting too stretched. And if you don't go, eventually the contractions will become so strong you won't be able to hold it!

Does eating chocolate cause acne?

No, but worrying about eating chocolate can. There is no evidence acne is caused by eating chocolate, but a group of dermatologists who studied 22 college students found emotional stress was directly linked to bad acne.

Should you put steak on a black eye?

Only if it's very cold. There is no magic in beef to help a battered eye, but coldness and pressure can help reduce bruising and swelling. So a big lump of ice would be just as good.

Why do drunks snore so loudly?

Alcohol increases snoring by relaxing the muscles that hold your throat open, allowing the soft palate tissue and uvula to flutter more as air passes.

Will whisky cure a cold?

Advertisements in the 1920s told us 'Guinness Is Good For You', but there is little evidence that it's true. 'Remedies' such as whisky, brandy and port probably just help you to forget how bad you feel.

Why do you see stars when you're hit on the head?

This doesn't only happen in cartoons – it's a sign of concussion. The stars appear when the occipital lobe – the part of your brain responsible for seeing – bangs on the inside of the skull.

Is sperm nutritious or fattening?

You won't get very fat by eating sperm. The average ejaculate (about one teaspoonful) contains 2–300 million sperm, but only about five calories. These come from protein and sugars that give the sperm the strength to swim. Other good stuff found in semen includes water, vitamin C, citric acid, phosphate, bicarbonates, zinc and prostaglandins.

Why does hair turn grey?

Every hair on our heads has cells containing the dark pigment melanin. These gradually die as we get older, turning the hair a more transparent colour such as grey, silver or white.

BIG hands, big **?**

There is no evidence that penis size is in any way linked to hand size, foot size or anything else. Two scientists measured the stretched penises of 104 men and compared the results with their shoe sizes, but found no relationship at all.

Chapter 32

POTTY ABOUT POTTER

Hold on to your broomsticks as you are dazzled with these amazing facts about the world of wizards.

There are only 1,000 first editions printed of the original *Harry Potter And The Philosopher's Stone*. Each one is now worth more than £20,000.

A toy firm has axed a vibrating replica of Harry's broomstick after mums complained their daughters spent too long riding it. Makers Mattel advertised the battery-operated toy as having 'a grooved stick and handle for easy riding'. One mum in Birmingham said: 'You have to wonder what an earth they were thinking of.'

The third Harry Potter film – *The Prisoner Of Azkaban* – has clocked up the greatest number of bloopers of any film released last year with a whopping 232 continuity errors, almost four times more than the closest contender, *Spider-Man 2*.

If all the published copies, hardback and paperback, in all translations, of the six Harry Potter books were laid flat, edge to edge, they would entirely cover Brazil.

In the second book, *Harry Potter And The Chamber Of Secrets*, Nearly Headless Nick is revived with Mandrake Potion – but ghosts can't eat or drink.

Author J.K. Rowling wrote ten different versions of the first chapter of *The Philosopher's Stone*.

J.K. Rowling wrote her first story – about a rabbit – when she was five and used to tell her pals stories at school lunchtime.

She came up with the names of the Hogwarts school houses – Hufflepuff, Slytherin, Gryffindor and Ravenclaw – on a plane and scribbled them on a sick bag.

Funnyman Stephen Fry made broadcasting history when Radio 4 aired his uninterrupted reading of *Harry Potter And The Philosopher's Stone*. It lasted eight-and-a-half hours.

Rowling admitted she found the penultimate book so hard to write that she even considered breaking her own arm at one stage.

Only one football club is mentioned in the first six books, West Ham United.

When trying to sell the first book, Rowling was so poor she had to type two copies of the manuscript because she couldn't afford to photocopy the original.

J.K. Rowlings's fortune is estimated at a bank-balance-busting £500 million – enough to buy 125,000 top-of-the-range Porsche Boxsters.

All of Wales could be covered in linoleum floor tiles using the amount of adhesive that sticks all the pages of the first six Harry Potter volumes.

Dumbledoore is the head of Hogwarts School, but did you know that his name means 'bumblebee' in Old English?

Students at the famous Hogwarts School catch the Hogwarts Express on 1 September every year. Classes always start next day, which is always a Monday. Now that's magic, as 2 September is normally on a Monday only once every six years.

The Hogwarts official motto is Drago Dormiens Nunquam Titillandus. – Latin for: 'Never tickle a sleeping dragon'.

Producers of the penultimate Harry Potter movie annoyed fans with a mistake on a tombstone. In the original publicity shot for the film, the dates on the inscription read: Tom Marvolo Riddle 1915–1943. But Potter's arch enemy wasn't born until 1926.

When the first Harry Potter book came out in 1997, J.K. Rowling's publisher told her: 'You'll never make any money out of children's books, Jo.'

There is a total of 717,800 words in the first five books, making J.K. Rowling's earnings a staggering £1,393 per word.

The three Potter movies so far have racked in a massive £1.35billion.

Book five in the series – *The Order Of The Phoenix* – sold 1.8million copies in the UK in 24 hours.

More than 265million Harry Potter books had been sold in 200 countries up to the release of the final instalment, *Harry Potter And The Deathly Hollows*.

The Hogwarts Express leaves from platform 'nine and three-quarters' at King's Cross station in London. This is based on the legend that the body of ancient Celtic leader Queen Boadicea is buried under what is now platform 10.

Chapter 33

CAN'T GET YOU OUT OF MY HEAD

Why is it always the worst, most sickly, irritating and annoying songs that work their way into your head and refuse to shift? Sometimes you end up humming them for days and days until you want to smash your head on the wall to stop it. So, read on if you dare.

'The Birdie Song' – The Tweets
With a little bit of this and a little bit of that and shake your bum... And do you remember the moves that went with it? Maddening, wasn't it? Got to No.2 in September 1981.

'Shaddap You Face' – Joe Dolce Music Theatre
A karaoke favourite. Says it all. Only play when drunk. Reached No.1 in February 1981.

'Grandad' – Clive Dunn
They don't like it up 'em, as Clive Dunn was famous for saying on *Dad's Army*. But they probably ran away even faster when they heard this sickly mush that got to No.1 in November 1970.

'Chirpy Chirpy Cheep Cheep' – Middle of the Road
'Woke up this morning and my momma was gone. Ooh wee chirpy chirpy cheep cheep.' You can hardly blame her. This teeth-grinding ditty reached No.1 in June 1971.

'Who Let The Dogs Out?' – Baha Men
Not everybody hated this when it made No.2 in October 2000. Posh and her pals loved singing it every time Jordan came into the room.

'Sugar, Sugar' – The Archies
For people desperate to be sick. Lyrics just keep repeating 'Ah sugar, ah honey honey, You are my candy girl, And you've got me wanting you' over and

over until everyone loses the will to live. Camped in the charts for 26 agonising weeks in 1969, including eight at the top.

'Because We Want To' – Billie

Before she got a full-time job as Dr Who's sidekick, Billie became the youngest-ever debut artist to reach No.1 when she was just 15 years and 287 days old. That was in July 1998, but it's just as annoying today.

'Achy Breaky Heart' – Billy Ray Cyrus

Not only did this song reach No.3 in July 1992, it also sparked something just as irritating – a line-dancing craze.

'Rat Rapping' – Roland Rat Superstar

Kids loved the puppet vermin and it shot to No.14 with this in November 1983.

'Itsy Bitsy Teeny Weeny Yellow Polka Dot Bikini' – Bombalurina & Timmy Mallett

The original 1960 version was OK, but coming from a grinning children's TV presenter in multi-coloured glasses, it got up more noses than the common cold on its way to No.1 in July 1990.

'Macarena' – Los Del Rio

Great to dance to when you've drunk so much you can barely stand... but who wants to listen to it? Someone did, as it reached No.2 in July 1996.

'Two Little Boys' – Rolf Harris

He was ace at drawing cartoons with a 6-inch paintbrush, but Rolf insisted on singing sickly songs like this one that stayed at No.1 for seven long weeks over Christmas 1969. 'Two little boys had two little toys...' Make it stop!

'(Everything I Do) I Do It For You' – Bryan Adams

Catchy song that went to No.1 July 1991. But then it stayed there. And stayed there. For sixteen bloody weeks until everyone in the country wanted to smash every copy with a sledgehammer.

'There's No One Quite Like Grandma' – St Winifred's School Choir

Somehow, this nauseating song by a squeaky-clean girls choir about how much they love their granny reached No.1 at Christmas in 1980.

'Fog On The Tyne (Revisited)' – Gazza and Lindisfarne

Now every time you hear this great Geordie favourite, the moment is spoiled by the memory of big, daft, grinning Gazza making this mockery of a remake with the group Lindisfarne, who should have known better. Toon Army soccer fans lifted it to No.2 in November 1990.

'Mr Blobby' – Mr Blobby

Noel Edmonds's cringey creation made you sick just looking at it, so when it started to warble too, well… Yet it reached No.1 at Christmas 1993.

'Boys (Summertime Love)' – Sabrina

With her gigantic boobs and sunny smile, no one could forget Sabrina. Or her terrible song that reached No.3 in June 1988.

'Just Say No' – Grange Hill Cast

After Zammos's heroin addiction storyline in the kids' soap, the Grange Hill crew released this anti-drugs anthem. The class effort gets an A grade – A for annoying. Got to No.5 in April 1986.

'Cheeky Song (Touch My Bum)' – The Cheeky Girls

Reached No.2 in December 2002 after the saucy pair shot to fame auditioning for *Popstars*.

'Star Trekkin' – The Firm

'Klingons on the starboard bow... Beam me up, Scotty!' Funny, but dreadful. Reached No.1 in June 1987.

'Rabbit' – Chas and Dave

Cockney funnymen Chas and Dave gave us this song with the memorable chorus: 'Rabbit, rabbit, rabbit, rabbit, rabbit, rabbit, rabbit, rabbit, rabbit, rabbit, rabbit, rabbit.' in 1980. It only got to No.8 but hung around like leftover stew.

'Whispering Grass' – Windsor Davies and Don Estelle

Comedy spin-off from the sitcom *It Ain't Half Hot Mum* reached No.1 in May 1975. It ain't half awful, Mum, more like!

'Fast Food Song' – The Fast Food Rockers

A great advert for Kentucky Fried Chicken and Pizza Hut, but a terrible song. No.2 in June 2003.

'Teletubbies Say "Eh-Oh"' – The Teletubbies

Everyone loved Po, La La, Tinky Winky and Dipsy, those bloated kids puppets who did nothing but squeak. Didn't they? Someone must have, as this reached No.1 in December 1997.

'Mysterious Girl' – Peter Andre

Peter Andre was irritating long before he made your toes curl by canoodling with Jordan on *I'm A Celebrity*. He reached No.2 with this catchy love song in September 1995.

'The Chicken Song' – Spitting Image

The plastic puppets drummed up this treat and got to No.1 in May 1986.

'Swing the Mood' – Jive Bunny and the Mastermixes

The cartoon bunny had a string of hits starting by getting to No.1 in July 1989.

'Anyone Can Fall In Love' – Anita Dobson

The Queen Vic's favourite landlady in *EastEnders* sang this to the theme tune of the soap, and got to No.4 in August 1986. You can see why Den divorced her.